PREPARING FOR TRIAL

60 DAYS AND COUNTING

PREPARING FOR TRIAL
60 DAYS AND COUNTING

BRUCE W. FELMLY

AMERICAN BAR ASSOCIATION
Defending Liberty
Pursuing Justice

FIRST
CHAIR
·PRESS·

Cover design by Andrew Alcala/ABA Design.

Printed in the United States of America.

19 18 17 16 15 5 4 3 2 1

ISBN: 978-1-63425-000-9

e-ISBN: 978-1-63425-001-6

Library of Congress Cataloging-in-Publication Data
Felmly, Bruce W., author.
   Preparing for trial : sixty days and counting / Bruce W. Felmly.
      pages cm
   Includes bibliographical references and index.
   ISBN 978-1-63425-000-9 (softcover : alk. paper) -- ISBN 978-1-63425-001-6 (e-book) 1. Pre-trial procedure--United States. 2. Trial practice--United States. I. Title.
   KF8915.F47 2015
   347'.7372--dc23   2014048266

To Susan—for her encouragement, patience,
support, and perspective, as my partner in life
and in the rigors of trial practice.

Contents

Foreword   xi

Introduction   xiii

Chapter 1
The Case Is Going to "Go": Setting the Stage for Trial Preparation   1
     Teamwork   3
     Preparation and Balance   4
     The Model for Our Discussion   5

Chapter 2
Day 60 to Day 30   7
     Scheduling   8
     Flyspeck the Case: Get It into Shape   10
     Testing, Demonstrative Evidence, Animations, "Day in
         the Life" Videos   13
     Planning Trial Presentation Techniques   15
     Mediation, Insurance Coverage Issues, and Mock Trials
         and Focus Groups   23
         Mediation and Settlement Negotiations   24
         Insurance   26
         Mock Trials and Focus Groups   26

Chapter 3
Day 30 to Day 20   29
     Preparing the Pretrial Filings   31
         The Pretrial Statement   32
         Views   34

Exhibit Lists 37
Depositions to Be Presented to the Jury 38
Timing of Opening Statements and Closing Arguments 40
Witness Lists 40
Prospects for Settlement 41
Trial Counsel 42
Waiver of Claims or Defenses 42
The Rest of the Pretrial Package 43
Proposed Jury Instructions 43
The Special Verdict Form 43
Requests for Findings of Fact and Rulings of Law 44
Motions in Limine 45
Requests Related to Voir Dire 48
Establishing the Trial Schedule 50
Prepare a Draft of Your Opening Statement 53

Chapter 4
Day 20 to Day 10 57
Final Pretrial Conference 57
Marking Exhibits and Resolving Objections 63
Preparing the Client for Trial 65

Chapter 5
Day 10 to Day 3 71
Prepare for Jury Selection 71
Preparing Your Witnesses 74
The Direct and Cross-Examination Outlines 74
Witness School 83
Logistics 87
Take Care of Yourself 89

Chapter 6
Day 3 to Day 0 91
The Final Weekend 91
Assembly of the File 91

Provisioning   92
Polishing the Opening   93
The Morning of the Trial   93

About the Author   97

Index   99

Foreword

In these days of the "vanishing trial," when there are ever-fewer opportunities to learn at the feet of masters, this book will be invaluable to guide trial lawyers—but especially those with fewer times at bat—to focus, prioritize, and prepare for that morning when they are called upon to say "Ready, Your Honor."

Whether one is counsel for plaintiff or the defense, in a larger case or a smaller one, the essential process of preparing in the final months before trial is the same, notwithstanding the fact that every case is unique, every court has different rules, and every judge has personal preferences. In recent years, detailed trial rules have proliferated in our jurisdictions, just as the tolerance, by courts and judges, of ignorance (or knowing non-compliance) of those rules has lessened. When these facts are coupled with client expectations, there is precious little room for "learning by doing" in preparing a case for trial.

You need this book to systematize your approach to the final weeks before trial, to assure there are no loose ends in your case, and to limit the stress of a very stressful time.

Bruce Felmly has been there. He has tried scores of cases in courts across the country in a career that has spanned more than 40 years. His text is spiced with personal anecdotes that demonstrate his humanity and provide you the reader with some comfort that another person has experienced the highs and lows of life as a trial lawyer.

I have gotten to know Bruce as a member of a remarkable fellowship of courtroom lawyers from across the continent. Bruce and I, along with others in that group, also share a passion for fly fishing. This pursuit has taken us from the salmon rivers of Labrador to Tierra del Fuego in Argentina. The demands of trial work and the intensity, laughter, camaraderie, and tall tales of the fish camp blend well, all adding to the perspective Bruce brings to this book.

In the course of his four decades as a trial lawyer, Bruce has been honored by his peers for his accomplishments as a trial lawyer. Among many accolades, he has been elected to Fellowship in the American College of Trial Lawyers and is a perennial Super Lawyer. He serves as head of the trial department of McLane, Graf, Raulerson & Middleton, P.A., the largest law firm in New Hampshire.

—Paul Fortino

Introduction

I learned how to try cases in the courtrooms of New Hampshire. On my first day of work in August, 1972, I was given several files by partners with years of trial experience. Over the months we prepared those cases for trial and tried some of them. My mentors carefully watched and corrected my initial forays in giving pre-view statements, arguing jury instructions in chambers, and handling the courtroom examinations of what a trial lawyer friend used to call "The Little People"—the nurses, friends of the plaintiff, the ambulance driver, the police officer—the witnesses who helped the storytelling of the case, but presented no great risk to a novice. Cases went to trial frequently and with wide variety—personal injury plaintiff cases, restrictive employment covenants, construction claims, teacher discharge cases, each offering opportunities for a young lawyer to present a case in a courtroom. Now, forty-three years and scores of trials later, the opportunities for the exceptionally talented young lawyers I mentor to gain trial experience are less common. When trials occur, they tend to last longer, and the financial and personal stakes for the individuals and companies we represent are often immense. The rules of court, expansion of discovery, proliferation of experts, and pretrial labyrinth of dispositive motions, motions in limine, and electronic discovery and evidence, all present a highly complex and dynamic playing field as the trial event approaches.

I have been fortunate not only in trying a large number of cases, but in the wide variety and different venues of those cases. As I began to try cases on my own in the late 1970s, without the safety net of the senior partner sitting at counsel table, the cases continually increased in complexity. Medical negligence and product liability claims for plaintiffs became a steady diet, providing the most demanding standards of pretrial organization and coordination. Commercial and business cases, often with multiple parties and rapidly escalating stakes, brought with them new technology, cost, and the management of extensive document discovery. Technology also presented the more experienced trial lawyer with new tools and techniques—video depositions, trial presentation software, exciting animation of accidents, and the use of Internet resources in preparing for expert cross-examinations and jury research.

The volume and complexity of the trials also reflected a change in nature of the cases. New opportunities arose to represent defendants in product liability cases, toxic tort environmental claims, and a wide array of claims for environmental clean-up costs among responsible parties and insurance carriers. Trials expanded to multi-week events focused on scientific proof, elaborate demonstrative evidence, and expert witnesses of every conceivable discipline and profession. The stage expanded from New Hampshire to courtrooms in Missouri, New York, Connecticut, Massachusetts, South Carolina—collectively described in our parochial New Hampshire view as "Away."

The goal of this handbook is to attempt to provide the inexperienced trial lawyer with the benefit of some of the things learned along the way, focusing on precise methods, procedures, techniques, best practices, and tricks that I believe are helpful in successfully preparing a case for trial. The commentary and technique represented here will be detailed and opinionated. This is a how-to handbook. We all know preparation is the key to success as a trial lawyer. This handbook will share my experiences, and what I have learned from others far more gifted, and to assemble these tips and approaches into a time-sensitive and flexible model that can be adapted to almost any type of trial. It goes without saying that a generalized approach to a discipline that is dependent on local court rules, customs, and practices in different states, federal versus state forums, and civil versus criminal cases, runs the risk of being contradicted by the specific practices or requirements of the forum. You will figure that out—I am convinced after my experience trying cases in various jurisdictions and with fine trial lawyers from "Away" that the basic steps and organizational demands have a high degree of consistency. Often the local trial lawyer's admonition that "Bruce, we don't do it that way here. . . ." translates into a recognition that he or she has not thought about doing it differently. Nevertheless, I will try wherever possible to identify important variations of which I am aware, and I caution you to check every suggestion and recommendation against the requirements of your applicable rules and the body of law in the courts where you practice.

It is important, as you review the suggestions that I offer for trial preparation, that you are mindful of the rapid change technology is bringing to the trial of cases. In my firm's litigation department, we have a team of trial lawyers and paralegals working with enhanced use of computers in the courtroom. This goes beyond trial presentation or trial projection tools, which are already commonly used, but now includes iPads and other tablets, which provide file storage, note taking, and even witness outlines and related presentation aids. It is likely that those devices will evolve into a primary platform for trial work, and, eventually, be overtaken by something else that is newer, faster, better . . . .

I know some lawyers who have already mastered or are testing the limits of those devices and there is no doubt that the devices will proliferate and be highly valuable. As I write in this handbook about trial notes, notebooks, and "three ring binders," being tools deployed in the courtroom, we know the mechanics will change within a few years to a more electronic format. My deployment of electronics in the courtroom is heavily focused on presentation aids, and accessing discovery information or case data. The flexibility, visibility, and nature of witness outlines and organized advocacy notes can be deployed on a tablet, but I have not yet mastered this skill. Technical changes will unquestionably impact courtroom advocacy, but that process of innovation will itself be transitory. The use of new devices and platforms will continue to grow. However, the key organizational criteria and lightning fast flexibility demanded of a lawyer in the crucible of trial will remain.

There is something else important to say about the purpose of this book. Too often experienced trial lawyers are seen by those just learning their trial skills as calm, self-confident, masters of the craft. These are folks who deftly arise and enter the courtroom with an even heartbeat, a clear eye, and a precise plan for the commencing trial. I have met such people, but they are very few, and this book is not for them, or those of you who have been given such gifts. The first day of trial, or at least the predawn hours before the battle is joined, is always a time of terrible self-doubt, drained emotional resources, building tension, and disorganization, and—in truth—a sometimes desperate wish to be almost anywhere else, far from a hotel room thinking through the trial about to start and watching the illuminated watch dial as it counts down to the 5:00 a.m. wake up call. The fear and emotional demands of trial become more manageable with experience, but are always with you.

The acceptance and harnessing of that emotional power, even fear, into passionate and articulate advocacy, quick responses on your feet, reversal of tactics when plans fall flat, and the setting of an internal stopwatch as a cross-examiner who sets up the final and critical question of the witness for 4:27 p.m., is enabled and assured by meticulous, exhaustive preparation. Preparation simply gets you through. All the things you can plan, anticipate, mitigate, and implement with your able and hardworking team provide you the energy and confidence to help manage the stress, confusion, mistakes, and constant professional tension that comes with demanding trials. There is a reason we use this word "trial," defining a dispute resolution event or process in our courts, but also as a term defining a testing, a suffering, or experiencing of a hardship. Trials are hard, but remain a supreme test of our skills.

Finally, a point about perspective. Preparation will not only enable you to withstand the pressure, stress, and exhaustion of the process, it will sustain you in those times when you lose. Trial lawyers do enjoy and celebrate their victories—but few in my experience savor the victory or celebrate the win with the intensity, duration, or constant flashback that comes with a crushing defeat. Those darker moments are managed best with the assurance that you did the absolute best you could do. Doing the best you can is assured when you have a plan, a system, a method, and a discipline to turn that goal of excellence into effective performance.

I am hopeful that the methods and tactics I will describe here, learned in my trials, will make your experiences more successful and satisfying.

Chapter 1

The Case Is Going to "Go": Setting the Stage for Trial Preparation

Spring 1997—Manchester, NH. MON 4:38 a.m.—The digital display burns into your brain. No escape to sleep this time, unlike 1:43 a.m. and 3:05 a.m. you saw earlier. Turn off both alarms, an hour before the appointed time. The demand of the day hits you hard with what must be a quart of adrenalin. It's dark and it's cold and you would give almost anything to bury yourself under the blankets. "It's always like this," you think, "I'll be loose as a goose tomorrow . . ." But at this moment you are overwhelmed. Not even sure if you can do it. The schedule calls for 15 days . . . and you are already exhausted.

The confidence starts to come back with the hottest shower you can stand. The shoes were shined last night, first time in two months. Yes, a bow tie on the first day— something about a bow tie. A few lines of the opening in the kitchen, nobody up but the dog. The dog either likes the opening or is excited because she thinks we are going bird hunting since it's so early.

The car is loaded with the boxes, seats folded down for the blowups. They look good. You've worked on

1

this case for two years and it is prepared as well as you and your team can do it. It's time to go. As you drive to the courthouse you load in the Eagles tape, blast the volume and soon it has its effect—you're singing for all you're worth about ". . . Standing on a corner in Winslow, Arizona" . . . It's the first day of trial and, damn it, you're ready.

In the Spring of 1997, I opened an article on trial preparation in the New Hampshire Trial Bar News with this vignette.[1] I revised the article in 2009, incorporating many of the innovations and practices in trial work that had changed over the ensuing twelve years. While still more has changed since then, the stress and pressure of the first day of trial remains. Rules and procedures have adapted to new technology, motion practice has proliferated and greatly impacted trial practice, but the drama and demands of preparing for trial are a constant. I still set two alarms for the first day—the Eagles are no longer on a tape, but we are still in Winslow. There is a new dog, she refuses to hunt, but gets excited when we arise before dawn. The trial blowups are more often stored in a laptop my paralegal will bring to the court for an early morning practice run on the demonstrative evidence, but I still order poster board in bulk.

The themes of this handbook remain the same as my writing in 1997. Trying a substantial case requires meticulous organization over a period of weeks preceding the trial. There are lawyers who, no doubt, still pull their cases together in the last weekend, but they are not trying cases of the variety or difficulty we will discuss. They are probably not trying their cases well, and are likely paying an intolerable cost in tons of stress and disruption of their personal and professional lives.

---

1. Trial Bar News, Vol. 19, Spring 1997, Bruce W. Felmly, "Preparing for Trial—Thirty Days and Counting."

Teamwork

Trial work demands a high degree of teamwork. While this handbook will often describe actions and events as if I were the only one involved, those who I work with in and on trials know the value and reliance I place on teamwork. Depending on the size and complexity of the case, there will be an associate or partner in the second chair; a paralegal highly trained in assembling exhibits, managing depositions, and organizing video presentations; and sometimes a specialist in litigation technology, assisting in the retrieval and presentation of electronically stored evidence. Most often this team has worked together in prior trials and knows the duties, demands, and techniques to make the presentation of the case come alive and meet the time demands of the court, and the essentials of persuasion in a courtroom. They know how to adapt the courtroom facilities to evidence presentation, and how to navigate negotiations of marking, exchanging, and resolving objections involving hundreds of exhibits. It is essential that you develop such a team, train them well, and rely on them to empower you to lead that effort on your feet in the courtroom.

Managing a trial team demands a system of accelerating team meetings and checklists, as the days leading to trial move forward. Do not rely on spontaneity. Calendar those meetings for set times, have a team member prepare an agenda, involve all the team participants and listen to their suggestions, complaints, and comments, and fix things that are not working. Encourage your team to make the preparation process efficient, productive, and even enjoyable. Build in humor: sometimes I have sent movie clips from the Internet of heroic speeches from cinema on the night before a jury draw. Try the movie clip from Aragorn at the Black Gate from Lord of the Rings—Return of the King.

Sons of Gondor! My brothers! I see in your eyes the same fear that would take the heart of me! A day may come when the courage of men fails, when we forsake our friends and break all bonds of fellowship. But it is not this day. An hour of wolves and shattered shields when the age of Men comes crashing down! But it is not this day! This day we fight! By all that you hold dear on this good Earth, I bid you stand! Men of the West!

Sure it's corny, but great fun, even if it's not gender neutral.

Since much of this handbook is aimed at those without significant trial experience, I am also mindful that unlike my good fortune, many of you will operate as a "team of one." The task, steps, challenges, and tactics are the same when you try alone, but the burdens are far greater. I have often tried against single trial lawyers, many of whom struggled with all the data, organization, and planning of a major trial without adequate support. In such case, I would limit my team to myself and one other in the actual courtroom. Most of those single opponents did well, gaining strong respect from the jury, but they also meticulously worked from checklists and systems. It can be done well in a three- to five-day trial, but for a case longer than a week, some effort to recruit assistants should be strongly considered.

Preparation and Balance

The model for this handbook presumes we are entering a window which opens 60 days before trial. In 1997, that same window was 30 days, but court rules and the demands of significant cases now require an earlier final push. No matter, a key point remains—whether 60 or 30 days, you and your team cannot emotionally sustain an all-out preparation sprint for the entire race. You need to develop a pace and respite from the demands of "the case." There is of course a tension here— I advocate for intense preparation, but also must provide for rest, stepping away from the file, maximizing family time, and careful stewardship of the health and happiness of your team. Trial work is rarely a dash; it is more often a marathon.

Creating that balance must recognize that losing a hard fought case is so painful that when it is over you will inevitably ask, "Should I have worked harder? Done more?" This is where method and organizational rigor help answer that question or doubt. Developing a trial preparation system, and following it, provides you the efficiency and attention to detail likely to avoid the loss, confidence and calmness in moments of failure, and the ability to move on assured that you flat-out did your best.

The Model for Our Discussion

There is huge variation in the nature of cases that go to trial. The most obvious and important is, of course, the difference between jury trials and bench trials. Most of what we will discuss in this handbook applies to trials generally and you will easily adapt the techniques to particular settings. I have avoided the temptation to peg our model to the mega case—the multiparty three-month saga with elaborate technology, hundreds of witnesses, and hundreds of millions at stake. I have limited personal experience in such trials, and they often are governed by special rules and procedures.

In order to put the suggestions and teachings of this handbook in context, I will ask you to assume several factors or scenarios about the cases and settings that will provide a platform for our discussion.

- The case we will discuss as our model is substantial. It could be a large commercial case, or a serious personal injury or death case. The clients, or client representatives, are counting on you to succeed, and are highly engaged. The case has been pending for approximately 18 months, and discovery is largely complete. There are lots of exhibits on both sides. Dispositive motions have either been resolved, or if pending, are not certain to be ruled upon before we are in trial. It is a jury trial—and we will explore different scenarios in selecting a jury.

- The case has been mediated without success, but all hopes at settlement are not lost. It is expected the case will last approximately ten trial days. There has been significant exchange of electronically stored information, and the presentation of the case will involve the use of trial presentation software or technology by both sides.

- There will be filed a variety of pretrial motions, motions in limine, some focusing on challenges to particular witnesses or exhibits. Some will relate to various concerns with opening statements, jury selection, and details of trial. It is uncertain whether the court will rule before the case convenes.

- There will be a schedule of pretrial filings in the weeks immediately prior to trial. Exhibit lists, pretrial memoranda, briefs on specific issues of law, jury instructions, and designation of deposition portions to be read or shown on video are all specified. Exhibits will be exchanged and pre-marked with objections presented to the court. All of this will lead up to a pretrial conference with the court. This conference will cover a wide variety of issues, motions, concerns, possibility of settlement, and will demand a great deal of preparation.

- This is not your only case. During the projected trial period you have expert disclosure deadlines with detailed reports due in two other cases, an appellate argument on projected day 8 of trial, and your 25th wedding anniversary, with family coming into town, on the second weekend of trial. You have your hands full for the next month or so.

Chapter 2

Day 60 to Day 30

The case had been pending for a year or more. My local counsel in that neighboring state had no real sense of the docket. The federal judge was notorious for combining a very rigid no continuance policy, with last minute trial scheduling. Once discovery was closed, we were fair game for trial assignment, and two weeks' notice was luxurious on his docket.

The notice arrived late in the week; the jury will be drawn on the Monday a week and a half out. The court was expecting that we would be a "draw and go." No continuances. Scheduling was a nightmare; our infectious disease expert was scheduled for a presentation that entire week in Chicago, proclaiming his attendance was "impossible." That means "very expensive." I had another trial scheduled in Manchester, New Hampshire, which would conflict with this case if it lasted longer than one week. The trial order specified that counsel should be sure there was no wasted portion of the trial day—we would invariably go from 9:00 a.m. to 4:30 p.m. You were expected to have all your witnesses ready to go and fill the entire day.

Jury selection was almost comical. Juror No. 8 reported she knew the lead defense lawyer, "Joe," and in fact went to a school prom with him. The judge spoke to the jurors in open court, but took objections and challenges at side bar, with the stage whispers of those discussions echoing in the courtroom. "I think she can be fair—they were only 14, for heaven's sakes." Joe smiled slightly, no doubt remembering her corsage. There was an existing defense firm client on the jury—he also knew "Joe"—and reportedly he too could be fair.

The trial began, the defense waived cross-examination of the first three family witnesses I put on, so we ran out of witnesses at about 3:10 p.m. (". . . Mr. Felmly, don't let this happen again.").

It was a challenging first day of trial.

Scheduling

Ideally, the preparation and organization of a major trial works toward a scheduled trial date, often set months ahead. In many jurisdictions, the week of trial, if not the day, is agreed upon at an early conference with the court dealing with structuring of the case. Witnesses, clients, and interested parties are all notified to hold that date far in advance. If the progress of the case slows, or the parties have legitimate reasons to adjust the schedule, more often than not it can be adjusted—at least once. An assigned date or an assigned week of trial provides a foundation for preparation that should be treasured. In the Day, such certainty was rare. Criminal cases constantly trumped the civil docket, judges riding circuit through New Hampshire counties did not have continuity or ownership of the case—*"Good morning, counsel. I have taken a look at the Pretrial Statements, but let's step back and make sure I know what I should tell this jury sitting out there about this case. We will get going on drawing our jury in a few moments . . ."* Counsel, parties, and witnesses, with poster boards, bankers boxes, and brief cases all stacked against the walls, would stand outside of the courtroom on the Monday when trials would begin, only to find out we might start Thursday, or how about September? In one case, in light of repeated promises by the clerk and judge, a client in a personal injury case was brought from her home in Scotland the weekend before trial; however, because the judge was called away we were advised the case would be continued for several weeks.

In many jurisdictions, variations of this uncertainty persist. Predictions of whether the case will be called are uncertain, and lawyers in those jurisdictions, as I used to, make numerous inquiries of the clerk of court or other counsel scheduled to try their cases on the same list. Everyone is trying to determine whether the case is really going to "go." A good portion of the rest of your time is spent apologizing to the clients and witnesses who marvel at such uncertainty in the scheduling of the critical event.

In this chronology of preparation and countdown to trial, try to make the most of having a baseline timetable or schedule you can rely upon. If you do not have it, it will demand so much more of your preparation, your state of readiness, and the goodwill of those who you rely upon to prepare your case. I encourage you to take the following steps as you approach the scheduling of the trial.

- Establish a realistic trial schedule within the limitations of the ability of the court to provide one. As the trial period approaches, develop good coordination with the clerk's office. Watch the docket and trial list for warning signs of conflict, delay, or postponement. Make sure you understand what's happening with the other cases on the trial list. Will the other cases settle?
- Notify all witnesses as soon as the trial period is established and make sure experts are holding those dates.
- Where uncertainty exists, or sudden assignment can occur, set the case up flexibly and have it in trial form as early as

possible. Pay special attention to the schedules of experts. Develop a good relationship with the clerk's office and trial judge, especially if you are from Away.

- Your opponent will also have these issues, try to work with her.

- Whenever possible, develop a relationship with opposing counsel which encourages cooperation and even trust in scheduling and handling administrative matters. The ability to achieve this, of course, varies greatly , but more often than not, it can be done. Describe your proposed trial schedule, discuss availability or sequence of witnesses, accommodate travel or work schedules of witnesses, agree to call unavailable witnesses out of order, work out issues or problems with certain exhibits, and coordinate use of electronic equipment. And make sure the judge knows you are doing this.

Flyspeck the Case: Get It into Shape

A milestone date of 60 days from trial provides adequate time to complete most remaining discovery, follow up on research or projects you have planned, and examine your evidence critically, shoring up weaknesses, filling gaps, jettisoning claims or approaches that have not proven workable. It is a time to stabilize and solidify what issues you are actually taking to trial, and who and what you are going to present as evidence. The process should be methodical and rigorous—with each team member participating in this planning effort. The following areas are a common focus for putting the case into shape for the push to trial.

- Assess all legal claims for viability. In drafting the Complaint, multiple counts and causes of actions were presented. Summary judgment may have reduced the array, but as we move to trial, it is time to make the hard decisions on the weak theories. Can you really prove the fraud claim—by the higher standard of proof demanded? Is the piercing-the-corporate-veil claim against the predecessor company a stretch? What about the negligence of nurses in the operating room, or against the primary care doctor who referred your client to the negligent surgeon? Why not focus on the critical defendants? Is the statutory Consumer Protection Act claim, with its lure of multiple damages and attorneys' fees, going to hold up, or, even if it gets to the jury, will it mandate a year or more of appeals with the likelihood of a bad outcome? What about the counterclaim—fine to return fire in the answer, but is it viable or does it now appear just spiteful? And how about those claims against the conveying landowner who appeared to perhaps know about the contamination before the property was sold? What about other people we seem to be leaving out? Does the information learned in discovery mandate adding new parties? Is it too late because of the amendment deadline, or the scheduling orders, or the statute of limitations? This is the last chance to assess whether the case needs to be reconfigured, and sometimes that is mandatory, even if it necessitates a several-month push back in the trial.

- Solidify and refine expert opinions. Most courts have rules, accepted practices, and sometimes even statutes that specify the requirements for expert proof. (See, for example, Federal Rules of Civil Procedure F.R.C.P. 26(e)(2)—Supplementation of expert opinions—30 days before trial.) Presuming you have properly disclosed your retained experts, provided reports as may be required and, if expert discovery is permitted, presented them for deposition— did their opinions hold up? Was the testimony elicited consistent with the standard of proof—"probably," "reasonable standards of certainty," or comparable burdens?

Did the expert ultimately disavow her expertise on some aspect of the case? *Question: Dr. Jones, now as I understand your report and CV, you do not hold yourself out as an "expert" in brain surgery—correct? Answer: "That is correct, I am not an expert."*

Do you now need to do more to clean up unnecessary or naïve concessions by the witness, or even decide to bring a new expert on board to shore up the gap? If you are going to supplement the opinion of the expert, or disclose new testing or research that may materially change disclosed opinions, this is the outer limit to make such a supplementary disclosure. In medical cases, be especially watchful of recently published reports or studies in high profile medical journals or changes in the plaintiff's medical condition. Beware of efforts by your expert, or your opponent, to assemble empirical data drawn (it will be claimed) from that testifying expert's own patients. Such home-grown testing, photos of patients, anecdotal assessments, miracle cures, and the like have a potentially powerful impact on jurors and raise lots of concerns, and a basis of challenge due to the inability to conduct discovery on those actual patients. Very few of those patients will want to sign up for having their medical records profiled by their treating surgeon in some remote trial.

Determine the extent to which rebuttal of the opinions of the opposing expert may require disclosure now, rather than holding your fire until the crucible of trial. Often it is essential to wait based upon trial tactics, but you need to assess the probable reaction of the trial judge who is weighing your duty to supplement your opinions. If it is *your* expert driving the direct testimony that will unveil the rebuttal, rather than your cross-examination of the opposing expert—watch out. Know the rules in your jurisdiction on marking or not marking exhibits expected to be used only in impeachment.

Testing, Demonstrative Evidence, Animations, "Day in the Life" Videos

Nearly every jury trial will benefit from persuasive and interesting demonstrative evidence. Mix your media. Jurors are immersed in television and other media that inform them with video, CSI forensics, and elaborate simulations of accidents or plane crashes within moments of a tragedy. They will appreciate and expect you to present at trial with such exciting and persuasive technologies.

But these things take time, are often expensive to produce, and require close coordination with your experts. They require precise assembly of the facts, the record, the dimensions of the accident scene, the laws of physics, and management of the arithmetic and technology essential to the creation of an admissible visual or audio product. In a complicated auto product liability case, will you purchase and bring into the courtroom an exemplar vehicle? Can you find one of the correct year, comparably equipped? How will you get it up the stairs to the courtroom, which was so magnificently appointed when the building opened in 1874? Will you conduct a test on how the laser surgical device at issue in the case actually cuts through human tissue? Would the court even allow you to use cadavers in the courtroom? Is it safe ("You are planning to do what? With a laser in my courtroom?!")? Would you risk failure if the device malfunctions or exhibits the dangers claimed? Will the glove "fit?"

Often testing or demonstrative re-creation is a matter of employing video *outside* the courtroom. Film the demonstration. The exemplar auto can be brought into the courthouse parking lot on a trailer for a court conducted "View" for inspection. The point is, these issues involve great expense and coordination with opposing counsel and the court's staff. This is the time to sort all that stuff out.

Animations present unique issues when they move beyond a generalized visual depiction of an incident or accident (a video "chalk" you might argue) and take on a claim of depicting scientific or engineering truth. A simple artist's rendition of a chain-reaction automobile accident (even with appropriate measurements ensuring the scale of the scene) is easy to do, and generally easy to get before the jury, whether or not it is marked as a full exhibit. By contrast, the animation of labor in childbirth, integrating the precise timing and medical data of a fetal heart monitor strip, with visual depiction as to the baby's descent through the birth canal, incorporating cross-reference to the nurse's notes and vital sign measurements, demands meticulous expert support.

Animations or other complicated demonstrative evidence should not be sprung belatedly on your opponent. This is not just because is it unfair, but also because there is a high risk that a last minute presentation of such a product might be excluded. This is especially true when the demonstrative incorporates assumptions or data that requires checking by your opponents and their experts. Your concerns that earlier disclosure may result in better preparation, rebuttal demonstratives, or motions to limit your demonstration are all real. On the other hand, disclosure two weeks before trial, or even earlier in unique cases, largely eliminates the surprise argument. Negotiations over content can proceed. The judge will likely say, "Look, you folks have several weeks to try to resolve these issues. Something is going to be presented to the jury and I have confidence you can come to agreement." When that hope is a pipe dream, consider preparing an early motion in limine seeking an affirmative ruling on the exhibit—referencing the cost of production, the efforts being made for meticulous accuracy, your efforts to gain assent, and the need for the court to rule in advance of trial.

Similarly, but more common, is the preparation of demonstrative video showing damages, such as "day in the life" films.

These involve video or photo collages intending to reflect pain and suffering, disability, rehabilitative care, disruption of family relationships, and general loss of enjoyment of life. The concerns with such evidence will often arise over redundancy. Court: ". . . counsel, 168 photos of the Jones family struggling with Mrs. Jones life as an amputee is just too much. Pick your best 30 photos, hopefully showing different activities and impacts . . ." At 60 days out, you should be working with your videographer if you are creating high-quality video presentations, with scripts and shooting lists of witnesses, and selection of venues all being carefully reduced to a story board or shooting script. The videographer knows there may be editing on the fly in the days before trial due to challenges or rulings, but you need to get this filmed.

Planning Trial Presentation Techniques

The decision of how your team will present evidence in the courtroom and to the jury should be decided now. You have enough time to plan for it, but you need to create a protocol. It will, of course, likely end up being a combination of various techniques, but establishing the level of technology is essential to your work in organizing, formatting, and coordinating with your opponent and the court staff on the presentation of the case.

There are essentially three variations in presenting evidence to a jury in trial. Most simply, and traditionally, the case can be presented without video enhancement. Witnesses are shown documents marked as exhibits in the witness box, jurors watch the witness look at the document or photo, sometimes the trial judge has a "bench book" or workbook of exhibits and he or she can read along. In some cases, the parties prepare notebooks or packets of some or all of the exhibits for each juror and they can read along. In any case, the document is reviewed by the witness, there is testimony, and then the exhibit is put back in the stack and the process moves on to the next document.

If the plan is to use hard copy exhibits without simultaneous display to the jury, counsel should strive to pre-mark those exhibits and resolve objections before the examination begins, whenever possible. The delays in trial and frustration of the jury watching lawyers walk over to the exhibit stack, present the document to the witness for identification, lay the foundation for obviously admissible documents, receive the "no objection" from the opponent, hand the document to the court reporter, who affixes the label to the exhibit, returning the document to the lawyer who presents to the witness for substantive discussion are time-consuming and unnecessary. This process has been taught to lawyers for generations and many of them follow it religiously, but it is tedious. The use of pre-marked exhibits with simultaneous video presentation to the jury cuts the total time of trial by at least a third, and probably in half, in my experience.

Enhancement of this process or a subset of the traditional trial now likely involves the use of "blowups"—important documents, photos, excerpts, or other presentations that are copied and pasted onto poster boards so that the witness, judge, and jury can all read them at the same time. One or more blowups with the critical contract language, accident photos, map of the property, and essential medical records often become a fixture in the courtroom during the days of trial, providing a constant basis of cross-checking and reference during the presentation of the evidence. They become wall hangings in the trial.

This traditional trial presentation, with limited visual enhancement, remains common and may be very well-suited to the themes or objectives in your case. Not surprisingly, this presentation is often favored by the party which does not want the jury to emphasize the contract language, accident scene photos, or the demolished vehicle.

The second general category or presentation technique involves moderate use of technology, at least for some of the evidence. This will typically occur by using some form of video overhead projector ("Elmo" device or document camera) where a document, picture, or object is laid on a tabular surface and a video camera positioned several feet above the object projects the exhibit onto a screen. The use of this type of device is especially useful for real-time drawing or "chalking" during the witness examination or argument. Oversized documents, maps, or documents you did not prepare to use in advance, are easily integrated into the examination by use of a document camera. Consider the following on-the-fly adaptation—

Witness: Actually, Mr. Felmly, that's not completely accurate. You may not be familiar with my 2007 article on stroke, where I said it was a foreseeable event with such symptoms. You have not shown me that article in our discussion here and I think it is important. (Mr. Felmly walks to the red well folder of articles in the medical research box behind his counsel table, pulling out the 2007 article and returning to the podium. During this period, the paralegal is toggling the electronic switch to power up the Elmo device, disconnecting the laptop presentation setup.)

Mr. Felmly: Well Doctor, I do have that specific article here, and let's discuss that. Let me display it here on the document camera so the jury can see exactly what you did say then. Looking at the summary or abstract of the article beginning on Page 691—and let's zoom in on this paragraph so we can all clearly see what you actually said—here it is . . . "It is of course possible that stroke can occur in such circumstances, but the data and clinical research on this subject is highly controversial. "Isn't that what you said in 2007 and published in your professional journal? A highly controversial opinion?"

The Elmo device does not have the speed, precision of display, or ease of dual, split, or multiple contrasting images. It can also be clumsy to use under stress, as you try to get images centered, calibrate proper back lighting of radiological studies, and manage "hands on" display techniques. But it remains an effective and easy-to-use device. When you employ a document camera with other electronic formats, such as laptop-driven trial presentation software, you need to have a seamless ability to toggle from one device to the other. Plugging and unplugging with multiple lines and wires crossing the floor, is like trying to manage 50 feet of fly line on the front deck of a bonefish skiff as you stand, trying to cast to a sighted oncoming fish—eventually you get it tangled around your feet.

The moderate use of technology also commonly involves the use of PowerPoint or some comparable program which enables the presentation of arguments, "bullets" of evidence, or limited presentations of charts, drafts, and the like. These slides are easy to use, prepare, and present. While we are discussing it, let me say that *simple* PowerPoint slides are essential. Avoid the inherent desire to put too much detail, such as exact quotes and too many bullets, into the PowerPoint. I have been trained by media folks to use a medium blue background color with yellow writing on your slides. It projects better that way. No silly clip art, no law firm logos or advertising. Coordinate carefully on the use, placement, and operation of the projector with your opposing counsel.

The moderate use of technology will commonly involve document camera presentations of exhibits, as well as PowerPoint presentations in opening and closing arguments, and sometimes, in witness examination. Almost any courtroom can be easily adapted for such uses, requiring only that monitors or a screen be set up with appropriate visibility to the jury. Often, a separate, smaller monitor will be set up for the judge. Most courts have these monitors available, using them for video depositions, but if not, rent them.

The third major approach to trial presentation involves extensive use of exhibit projection, integrated video deposition clips, integrated PowerPoint-type slides for argument, and access and ability to draw upon the entire word-searchable file of not only the Plaintiff and Defendant exhibits, but all produced discovery. This type of presentation is basically laptop driven, but it is evolving into the use of iPads and other tablets. Commonly, in major cases, counsel employing such trial presentation techniques hire vendors or consultants not only to prepare or format the materials, but actually to operate the laptop and presentation in the courtroom during the trial. These folks are adept at preparing creative mixed-image slides, modifying or highlighting the exhibits in the wee hours of the morning, and other demonstrative techniques. The retention of such a consultant may be necessary in some cases with monumental numbers of exhibits or multiple parties in a joint defense case, integrating materials from different underlying databases. It may also be valuable to hire a media professional where the Plaintiff and Defendant agree on joint assembly and presentation of the demonstrative evidence. I have never successfully negotiated such a joint presentation agreement, probably because the opportunities for persuasive advocacy in presentation, zooming, and immediate switching to other exhibits are somewhat partisan and that tends to preclude sharing of technology consultants.

On the other hand, a well-trained and experienced trial team can readily prepare and present such evidence in a major trial, with complicated exhibits, drawing on law firm resources and capabilities. I will not describe all the details or techniques of such trial presentation software or media, but here are a number of considerations:

- Make sure all data is not only backed up against possible deletion or erasure, but can be formatted during trial if the equipment fails or you otherwise need a backup presentation mode. Have the data on a flash drive, on a backup laptop, and/or in online cloud storage so that you can immediately switch over to them if there is some problem with your equipment.

- Prepare and display your presentation with a kit containing adapters for different devices, suitable extension cords, and extra projection bulbs, all designed to deal with the potential for failure of the devices in the case. Everything that can go wrong, will go wrong. Test everything. Get permission to access the courthouse as long in advance of the first day of trial as possible to set up, and use noon recesses to fine-tune your presentation. Worry about the lighting and the ability of the jury to fully see the evidence. In some courts, you need to get the judge to order the access during the noon recess or before the trial day from the bailiffs. If you are trying in a court "Away," take the time to visit and inspect the courtroom prior to the trial, evaluating any available court technology systems. Judges and clerks who have courtroom technology invariably encourage the lawyers to explore and use it, so show interest, cooperation, and adaptation to their systems by testing it and making sure it will work for your case.

- Work with your team to create instantly available displays of all Plaintiff and Defendant exhibits. Put exhibits you intend to use in your direct and cross-examination of witnesses into separate files stored on the laptop for those examinations. If those exhibits benefit from highlighting, split-image comparison, or some other form of applied emphasis, have those enhanced exhibits prepared in advance and put into the examination folder. Alternatively, instruct your laptop operator (or learn personally) how to zoom in on an image, cut and paste the critical portion, or apply yellow highlighting. It is beneficial that at least at some point during the trial you actually do this yourself in front of the jury, making it clear that you, and not just your team members, are invested in how to operate these devices in order to present the case in an interesting way.

- Have the entire body of discovery produced in the case accessible through your laptop. This generally requires the integration or application of your underlying data management software (for example Concordance, Summation, and many others) with your trial presentation software. Trying to run them together can be very slow on the laptop and your operator should be trained in how to exit the presentation mode to search for the e-mail you remembered is out there somewhere in the hundreds of thousands of pages of documents. The goal is to be able to find it and present it in the next minute or two, and that requires laptop speed.

- Format your video depositions so that the deposition, or preferably, clips of key passages, can be presented with the printed text of the testimony displayed in synchronization with the soundtrack on the monitor. The ability to do this should be anticipated at the time the deposition is first scheduled and taken, and the video operator or the court reporter should understand your requirements and intentions for a synchronized software presentation when the video is displayed.

One of the most irritating and stressful problems of trial practice is the editing of video depositions on short notice, immediately prior to the display of the deposition to the jury. Long ago, this often involved the judge reviewing the objections to Dr. Smith's video during the noon recess, making rulings at 1:17 p.m. The retained videographer would then rush to try to edit out, kill the sound, or otherwise honor the court's ruling by editing, all during the 13 minutes left before the jury arrived after the lunch break. Digital presentation in the hands of an experienced team member, with synchronized video clips, makes this far less troublesome.

Determine if your particular court has implemented technology that utilizes "bar code" scanning of exhibits for display to the jury. I have tried one case using this technology, but it was many years ago. It was slow, sort of like the supermarket clerk who runs your Wheaties box three times under the scanner before he gets a hit, and it was somewhat cumbersome to operate. I am told it is now improved, but I am also told that using the bar code self-check-out line at Home Depot is easy. I still tend to avoid it, preferring a trained operator to scan my items as I check out. Then again, I recently checked in for a flight with a QR code boarding pass on my smart phone.

Treat your media operators with respect and kindness—patient at all costs when there is some glitch in the presentation.

I tried a multi-week jury case in a large Midwestern city where my opponent hired a video presentation consultant from the West Coast. He got special permission from our judge to wire the courtroom for multiple devices to bring this technology to the jury. He had a team of three to five associates and paralegals, plus the video guy, who happened to be very pleasant and adept. Lead counsel had never practiced with the presentation software and did not know its capabilities, even in the most basic applications of zooming or moving between various files.

On the first day of trial, on the first witness, opposing counsel struggled repeatedly with attempts to call up the exhibits. He could not tolerate a few seconds of delay while the exhibit was located by the operator and displayed. He had not provided the operator with a sequential list of exhibits to be displayed during the examination—each request to the operator was a surprise. I knew the case cold, but I could not figure out where opposing counsel was going from question to question and there was no way that the operator was going to know. Multiple whispered conferences occurred between the lawyer and the operator, with counsel's rising anger becoming a concern for the judge and the operator. After several hours of this display, counsel asked me if he could use my Elmo video projector, proclaiming to the entire courtroom that he was done with the "new-fangled technology." I got up, turned on the device, and tried to show him how to enlarge and zoom an image. I do not believe that he had ever used an Elmo. In the meantime, he was so flustered that he misplaced his legal pad with all of his direct examination notes and commissioned a several minute hunt for that treasure which had his team scurrying around the front of the courtroom. Eventually, Juror No. 2, in the front row, whistled to my opponent, and without saying anything pointed to the legal pad lying on the corner edge of the jury box. Bad start to the case.

Avoid such situations.

One last comment on the types of technology and forms of media or presentation: Wherever possible, try to employ a mixed-media approach. While jurors and judges appreciate the use of electronic presentation, and it saves valuable time, mixing in "blowup" charts on the key contract language, using flip charts and markers while the witness illustrates a point, or having a light box to display an original radiograph brings vitality and interest to the trial. Even in the most complex case, an all-electronic platform is usually a mistake, in my opinion.

Mediation, Insurance Coverage Issues, and Mock Trials and Focus Groups

The period 60 to 30 days out from trial provides the last realistic opportunity to address or implement a number of issues that have the tendency to distract from critical trial preparation if they are not undertaken at this time. Included here is whether further efforts are going to be expended on settlement, and specifically, whether a mediation, or increasingly a second mediation, will be organized and undertaken. This is also the time that a wide variety of insurance issues should be examined in the context of the approaching trial. And in the proper case, you and your clients may want to conduct a confidential trial simulation, presenting the case to pre-selected "jurors" who will provide feedback and identify problems, shoring up your confidence, or causing you to run for the hills.

Each of these topics, and others that may be unique to your case, requires thought, concentration, and expenditure of time and money, all of which will be in diminishing supply if not handled at this point. There are a variety of considerations that relate to these topics.

Mediation and Settlement Negotiations

We cannot get away from the reality that the high percentage of cases still settle on the courthouse steps, or sometimes, even during trial. I recall an examination in a bench trial of an expert, where I was interrupted by my corporate in-house counsel when he came into the courtroom, walked up to the podium from which I was examining, and slapped a yellow sticky note with writing on it directly on the black binder containing my witness outlines. He then retreated to his place in the pews behind the rail.

Judge: Mr. Felmly, would you like to share with the court what is going on and perhaps even what the note says?

Mr. Felmly: Certainly your Honor. I think this might be a good time for a short recess for me to further confirm the contents. The note says, "Bruce. Stop. Case just settled outside in the hall with defense corporate counsel."

Judge: It appears this is an excellent time for a brief recess. Thank you.

Mediation is so common now that its timing is routinely incorporated into case structuring plans or orders. Two months out from trial is a good time to mediate, especially if the disclosure of experts, rulings on dispositive motions, and general exchange of knowledge about the case has developed an ability of counsel on both sides to assess the risks of trial. Most often, enough has happened by this time to enable a realistic mediation. Many judges and many court systems either strongly encourage, or virtually mandate, mediation absent some strong advocacy proving that it is hopeless.

This timing also favors the ability to find a neutral with a proven track record but a very busy mediation schedule. Trial lawyers often agree on the identity of the "A-list" mediators and they are often not readily available on a week's notice as trial is about to commence. While all of these factors favor mediation 60 days or so out, how do you present this idea to your opponents or respond when they bring it up? It is easier if the court schedules a hearing and the judge asks why this cannot be settled in mediation. That may well happen at the final pretrial conference, opening the door for each side to embrace this proposal. But that conference remains more than 30 days away. In a jury trial case, the judge may suggest that he or she serve as a mediator or have another colleague on the bench do it. All of these approaches can work, or go very poorly, depending on the case, the clients, the judge, and the personality of your opponent. What is important is that you consider whether this timing is good and respond appropriately when you are at this point in preparation. In some cases, I have brought in talented partners to focus on settlement and mediation in the run-up to trial, explaining that I am in the final innings of preparation and essentially refuse to dilute my trial preparation efforts with the endless back and forth that some mediation or settlement sessions often demand. Some of that was for show I suppose, but some was a serious effort to stay focused. That may work for you.

Insurance

There are a variety of insurance coverage issues that can complicate things in the weeks before trial and which consume much time and energy. Representing a defendant with inadequate insurance requires a careful assessment of the trial risk, or worse, may require hard slugging with the carrier over denials of coverage and payment of defense costs subject to a reservation of rights. All of this will raise a variety of duties, responsibilities, and procedures that may impact your preparation of the case. Where there is inadequate insurance and there is the potential of an overage verdict, how is that risk is being managed? Is the carrier responding appropriately to settlement overtures? You need time to properly make a record with regard to these actions. Are there declaratory judgment actions pending? When will they be resolved and how will that impact the timing and reality of the upcoming trial? Will there be settlement negotiations and meetings with one or more carriers? Will you be involved in those and where and when will they occur? This is all critical to your client and distracting from your focus on the evidence and witnesses. Again, the assistance of a talented partner may help to avoid distraction during the throes of preparation.

Mock Trials and Focus Groups

I have some, not extensive, experience in using focus groups or mock trials in the effort to gain information or a probable jury reaction in a pending case. In their best sense, these exercises test reactions to certain evidence and arguments, and may help the development of theories. At worst, in a small state like New Hampshire, the confidentiality of the event may be compromised, unless extreme care is taken to select persons close enough to the area from which the ultimate jury will be drawn, but who will also maintain your secrecy.

In most instances, I find it very difficult for the jurors to believe that this is a real trial and I have the sense that it can become a popularity contest for the juries as to which lawyer presenter is best. Jury consultants and others who market this service have solutions for all of these issues—you will be told. I have also assembled my own mock jury panels, videotaped several during day-long sessions, and have had some success with them. They can be valuable, but they are a lot of work to prepare. Carefully orient your client on the advantages and limitations of mock jury panels and bring a high degree of confidentiality to the preparation.

If you employ a mock trial or focus group presentation, do not focus on who "wins" or "loses" in such an effort. Rather, test theories and evidence for resonance with typical jurors.

Chapter 3

Day 30 to Day 20

The run-up to the final pretrial conference began with a telephone call to a senior lawyer I had known for years. He had recently tried a case in front of my assigned judge on medical issues. I called him, explaining my case was coming up for trial in a month or so, I had heard some issues about this judge, but had no personal experience with him. The judge had a reputation. I explained briefly the nature of the case, my concerns over the relationship of one senior defense counsel that had been rumored to exist with this judge, and asked about his experience in his recent case.

Lawyer: "Do you drive a car?"

Bruce: "Yes, Jim, I drive a car."

Lawyer: "Well, I don't mean to be too dramatic, but I would suggest that you climb in it, try to find a deserted stretch of road where no one else will be driving, and take that car and at a moderate rate of speed, drive into a tree. That is likely to not cause serious injuries to you, but enough so that you'll be admitted to the hospital and have great grounds for a continuance."

Bruce: "Jim, it can't be that bad..."

Lawyer: "It's that bad."

The pretrial conference for this case was memorable. There were a number of motions that had been filed by the multiple defendants raising all kinds of issues about evidence that should not be allowed into the trial. They were strained, but the trial judge was intrigued with all of them. Toward the end of the conference, the senior lawyer who reportedly had a close personal relationship with the judge raised the issue that became the focus of the case at trial.

Senior Defense Lawyer: "Your Honor, I don't know if you've seen Judge Jones' ruling that permitted Mr. Felmly to obtain a copy of a confidential non-disclosed expert report, but something has got to be done about that. Mr. Felmly is now planning to subpoena the doctor who gave me a private, confidential report, frankly critical of the defendant in this case. He is subpoenaing that doctor to trial against his will and that's just wrong."

Judge: "Is that true, Mr. Felmly, are you really bringing in a medical witness against his will that defense counsel had consulted with confidentially?"

Mr. Felmly: "Not exactly. They put the very critical report of their client in front of their testifying expert who used it in his opinions. Judge Jones said that was a waiver of any privileges or work product and that I could obtain it on discovery."

Judge: "But it seems terribly prejudicial to me, Mr. Felmly."

Mr. Felmly: "It's certainly prejudicial, Your Honor. It shows that their case is indefensible, but it does get to the truth of the case. Even their defense expert found malpractice."

An hour-long argument ensued, the trial judge clearly showed his leaning for not permitting the witness to be subpoenaed "against his will" into trial. There was an agreed upon schedule to provide briefing to the Court on these issues. The case literally hinged on this issue and was changing at light speed.

Ultimately, the court ruled that the witness could not be compelled to confirm the opinions he had freely put into his report to counsel, critical of the defendant. The first trial resulted in a defense verdict. The holding on appeal opinion in the Supreme Court reversing this verdict began with the proposition that a trial is a "search for the truth. . . "

As I think about it now, the run-up to the pretrial conference and the way that was handled was dispositive. I would handle it today a bit differently, but it points out that very few things are more important than the 30 or so days before trial, when critical rulings are likely to be made that will shape or control the case.

Post Script—Some years later I was working at my desk when the phone rang and a lawyer I did not know from the North Country called to say that he was aware of my involvement with that particular judge in my trial and wondered if I could take a moment to talk about it. He was about to try a medical negligence case with that judge presiding and wondered if I had any tips or suggestions—

Mr. Felmly: "Do you drive a car?"

Preparing the Pretrial Filings

In almost any trial court, there are going to be an established set of required filings and actions that are part of the pretrial process and need to be submitted to the Court a month or so before trial. They will be the focus of the meeting with the judge some weeks before trial, a meeting called the pretrial or trial management conference. In the federal courts, the requirements will usually arise in local rules of the district court that will amplify and expand the general provisions set forth in Federal Rule of Civil Procedure 16. Comparing the procedure in a number of state courts, there is, of course, more variety, but the documentation and steps that I will describe here tend to be reflected in most courts in which I have been fortunate to practice.

Historically, these requirements were set forth in something called a "Pretrial Statement." Today, the Pretrial Statement tends to come with a companion set of related documents, all of which are properly focused on trying to organize the presentation of the case, identify particular issues for the resolution by the court, and give the court a head start with respect to its job in sorting out instructions to the jury and ruling on the admissibility of exhibits. We also now see a proliferation of motions bearing on trial evidence, most commonly "motions in limine," and they range in merit from wildly scattered complaints about particular pieces of evidence (usually to be denied as a matter of course) to sharply focused evidentiary challenges to testimony or exhibits presenting cutting edge issues. These motions, lists of witnesses, exhibits, identification of legal issues, together with a host of housekeeping questions or matters which will impact the efficiency of presentation in the case, will be raised in the filings which I refer to with my team as the "Pretrial Package." I will outline the principal issues below that are likely to arise in assembling these pleadings, evidentiary presentations, and argument.

Your own jurisdiction will, no doubt, have its own catalog of requirements, but this will alert you to the most important candidates for consideration.

The Pretrial Statement

The Pretrial Statement is certainly the ancestral foundation for today's Pretrial Package. It used to be that it was often the only document that was filed. It was intended to be perfunctory, general, and was not studied much by the trial judge. It described the essential nature of the remaining claims in the case, the approximate number of days of trial, and gave a list of witnesses that were expected to be called, which was often extremely general ("all doctors, nurses, chiropractors, police officers"). It also usually set forth some admonitions about not waiving certain requisites of proof, such as requiring the presence of authenticated records prior to admission into evidence. Lawyers and judges would conference ten days or so before the trial, discuss the probability of being "reached," and most problems with evidence and challenges to witnesses would await the actual trial. All of those items or issues remain part of a Pretrial Statement.

Today, however, the Pretrial Statement requires significantly more thought and attention. It will usually contain a specific statement of what claims may be waived or relinquished, a precise description of issues of law which may require specialized briefing, a description of the current status of settlement negotiations, and whether mediation is under consideration or has been held. It will also include statements regarding any necessary amendments of pleadings or other ministerial actions designed to clean up problems with the case (Are the proper names of all parties correct? Have people died? Do we have all the parties there or has there been some change in their corporate status or the like?) Sometimes the parties will stipulate to certain facts in order to simplify the trial and make things go more quickly. If there is a change in the demand for jury trial, and everyone is now willing to go with a bench trial, this will be the time and place when that is described or stipulated. If there are special or unusual defenses, you will want to be sure to spell them out and draw them to the attention of the court. Many Pretrial Statements require an itemization of various medical and special damages, sometimes with provisions on challenging the admissibility of medical bills. If you are going to be reading depositions into evidence, this is the point where you will identify them, with particular attention to whether you are going to present them on video. The pretrial statement will also indicate if either party requests a "view" by the jury of any location relevant to the trial.

Views

This is a good place to comment on the "view." In the Day, trials often started with everybody piling into a car or bus and heading off to the scene of the event with the jury to assess the scene and provide a platform or foundation for the evidence that was about to be presented. There would be a short orientation by counsel, the "pre-view statement," where the lawyers would tell the jury about the scene, without telling them the relevance of what they were seeing. For instance, "Please note whether or not there is a traffic light controlling the intersection at this location." Unfortunately, views seem to have fallen into disfavor in many courts. In some respects it is true that a video of the scene or photographs can provide necessary orientation for the jury as to the location of what happened and it probably saves some time. But in a substantial case, where the geography of the case event or the relationship of buildings, physical monuments, or even the proximity of one office space to another is important, there is no substitute for a view. Those judges who say that it is a waste of time, that the jury doesn't need to be dragged out there, respectfully, have it wrong. Counsel should urge a view in any case where it can legitimately be seen as important.

In my first year or so of practice, I tried a case with a senior partner defending our client, the telephone company. The case involved a lineman's truck, which was repairing telephone lines along the road, with orange cones placed around the truck. The plaintiff, with the car loaded with kids, came down the hill on an early spring day when there was slush and snow on the highway, approaching the scene where the lineman was working. She lost control of the vehicle, going off the road on the opposite side of the highway and hit a tree. She suffered a moderate injury in the collision, the kids were fine, but we tried that case for a week with legal questions involving the "instinctive action doctrine." A modest jury verdict for the plaintiff resulted after the trial court gave an instruction that basically postulated the existence of an emergency, telling the jury she could operate the car almost any way she wanted when she came down that hill and saw those cones on the side of the road. The case was reversed on appeal, finding the instruction wrong on the law.

As luck would have it, the new trial was scheduled on approximately the fourth anniversary of the original accident. It was April in New Hampshire, and it was snowing as the bus left the courthouse with the jurors, heading the fifteen miles to the view. As we arrived at the accident scene, the sheriff's deputy in charge of the view came onto the jury bus and explained to the jury that this was an extremely treacherous spot, that there was slush and ice on the road, that they needed to be extremely careful because there were oncoming cars hurtling down the hillside slope and he didn't want anyone killed at the scene.

I made eye contact with the trial judge who had gone along on the view, but did not ask for a mistrial at that point. For starters, it was clear the deputy was correct, the scene was treacherous, we were slipping all over the highway, and nothing good was coming from that view.

At approximately 9:30 that evening, the case was settled in a series of phone calls involving in-house counsel, myself, and the plaintiff's counsel.

If you think a view is important, carefully explain why in the Pretrial Statement or in another document that is going to get the attention of the court. Budgets are sparse and it can be difficult to get the resources to transport the jury to the scene, but there is no substitute for a visual inspection. Most often the cost of the view is going to be borne by the party that requested it. If the view is of premises that your client controls, and the view will have an impact on the impression the jury will form of your client, make sure that the premises are in good shape for the view. This is not about distorting, changing critical evidence or facilities, or manipulating the scene, but in the same way we dress up for courtroom proceedings, it wouldn't hurt for the client to clean the living room and make the house presentable. Stop short of having the client baking fresh bread on the morning of the view, as realtors suggest when selling a home.

If the property is in the control of your opponent, make sure you take a look at the property *before* the actual view to make sure it has not been changed. I recall a case involving a race track accident during the Friday night races where, on the weekend before the view, the racetrack refurbished the grandstand, upgraded the safety equipment and fencing, and painted the trackside barriers to give the best possible appearance of a safe and well-maintained track. In such cases, you will be tempted to mention to the jury not to bump against the track safety wall so that they don't get paint on their jackets. Views in cases involving allegations of sexual harassment, assault, or a host of other misconduct raise interesting issues. Is the elementary school going to be emptied of students before the jury parades in to see where Mr. Black's classroom was and where the alleged assaults on the children took place? Views related to the inspection of machinery, automobiles involved in accidents, and other equipment involved in tragic events raise special problems. Has the equipment or debris been changed by weather, simple decay, or by intentional acts of one of the parties? Often having a photographic record of the scene at the time of the accident or event is important to correlate and maintain the accuracy of the scene at the time of the view.

You should also discuss with the court whether the jury is going to be able to ask questions during the view. They will, unless admonished to refrain. Judges have a wide variety of positions regarding this, premised in part on the fact that the view is properly being considered by the jury as evidence, but the statements of counsel at the view, orienting them at the scene, are not evidence. Question from Juror: "I notice that there are lights here in the barn. Can you tell me, Mr. Felmly, whether they were on at the time your client supposedly brought Mrs. Smith into the barn and attacked her?"

Views are powerful evidence; they make a strong impression on the jury, and they raise all types of both anticipated and unanticipated issues. Think through them carefully, work them out in the Pretrial Statement to describe what you propose will be the procedure and actual navigation through the view, and think about how you are going to handle questions or remarks made by the jury. Also, it is not uncommon for views to involve multiple locations, where the jury is taken from one place to another. Sometimes the sequence in which you present them is important.

Exhibit Lists

The Pretrial Statement generally requires a listing of exhibits proposed to be offered. Lawyers often assume that no one will challenge the fact that the plaintiff received a medical bill, that the police report will come in because it is a police report and it was filled out by a policeman, or that the doctor's medical record was received from the doctor's office and clearly must be covered by the exception to the hearsay rule involving medical diagnosis and treatment. Of course, nothing is quite that simple, and you need to assess your evidence carefully and critically to make sure that you are going to be able to get it in, or at least present to the court and your opponent, a proposal for how issues involving custodians and formalities of proof will be handled. The Pretrial Statement is a place to do that.

There is no substitute for knowing the hearsay exceptions and definition of hearsay inside and out. While it is true that medical records commonly come in to prove medical diagnosis and treatment, many emergency room records will extensively discuss the circumstances of the accident, all as presented by the family of the plaintiff in the minutes after the accident.

"Mrs. Jones presented to the emergency room by ambulance at 10:40 p.m. after being struck by a red Camaro traveling at a high rate of speed without operating lights on Jackson Street. She was dragged for approximately 80 feet, before slamming into a telephone pole, where she was found by the medical technicians summoned by a 911 call. At the scene, she reported that a white male with an Oakland Athletics baseball hat got out of the car and asked if she was okay. She now reports that she has a severe headache, an inability to move her lower extremities, and she's bleeding from her nose. During the physical examination. . . "

Many medical records go well beyond medical diagnosis and treatment and are open to challenge. Often the parties can agree on appropriate redaction and take care of these evidentiary objections, but not if they do not think about it in advance. The issue of medical bills and what is compensable in a trial is complicated by the fact that almost no one currently pays the exact amount of the medical bill. The hospital or physician commonly provides a bill for say, $500.00, and ultimately the insurance company or governmental provider pays something closer to $320.00. Innumerable battles result over the question of who absorbs the discount and what number goes to the jury. The court opinions on this are commonly inconsistent and, even in my own jurisdiction, different results prevail. Importantly, you need to understand that uncertainty, plan for it, and be in a position to present your evidence irrespective of which way the question is resolved.

Depositions to Be Presented to the Jury
If you know that a witness is going to be unavailable for trial, it is important to identify in the Pretrial Statement that a deposition of that witness will be read to the jury. In many cases, that will involve not only a written deposition being

presented to the court, but also the presentation to the jury of the deposition on video. The court will very likely require that the parties cooperate and try to identify the segments or sections of the deposition to be presented. There is an enormous temptation when you are preparing for trial to think that everything is invaluable and that the jury will hang on every word of the deponent, so nothing should be cut. This is almost always wrong. If you have a deposition that goes for approximately 60 printed pages (full pages—I'm not talking a condensed version with four pages per sheet for the moment), it is unlikely that you are going to be able to read that in court in 60 minutes. I talk fast and perhaps I can do that on video, but most people will find that those 60 pages of deposition will run 80 minutes of reading to the court and jury. That is a long time to have somebody read to you. Depositions are an increasing phenomenon in terms of trial evidence; judges are reluctant to recess the case or continue the entire trial because of the unavailability of witnesses. The case must go on, and often that means the presentation of depositions.

Video depositions have improved enormously over the years. Use them whenever possible. The synchronization of the transcript of the video with the actual recording is now virtually seamless, enabling both ease of editing, as well as comprehension by the jury as they observe both the witness on video and the text being portrayed beneath the video. It is far better than C-Span. Moreover, the use of digital presentation in the courtroom for depositions also enables display in the video of exhibits that are being referred to by the witness during the testimony. Thus, the video will show the witness holding the contract exhibit in her hand and being examined with respect to it, perhaps reading various sections, while a split image to the right side of the video screen can bring up the actual document (marked as Exhibit 4) and you can show the jury what the witness is reading.

Timing of Opening Statements and Closing Arguments

Most courts have a rule with respect to the length of Opening Statements and Closing Arguments. In my experience, the most common period is one half hour, and that is fine for many fairly routine cases. The Pretrial Statement is a place to ask for slightly more time. I almost invariably ask for 45 minutes in the cases that I am trying. Lawyers are notoriously bad at watching the clock while giving Opening Statements and Closings, but you must plan yours carefully, use moot court or practice sessions, and be sure the time of your Opening is calibrated.

I also suggest that you discuss with both your opponent and the court the fact that you will be using certain exhibits during your Opening. This, of course, presumes that the documents, photos, videos, and bloody handguns that you will be showing the jury during your Opening Statement are going to be admitted as full exhibits. The proper presentation of an Opening Statement requires that you either get an agreement as to the fact that a particular exhibit can be displayed, irrespective of the fact that it has not been fully marked, or get agreement from the other side that it can be marked as a full exhibit in advance of trial. What goes around comes around on these matters, and most of the time the things that you would want to show to the jury during your Opening Statement are going to be full exhibits. If that is not true with respect to something you want to show them in Opening, you likely have bigger problems with your case than what exhibits are going to get in or out. If you are using trial presentation software during your Opening Statement, it may be suitable to mention that in the Pretrial Statement and identify the types of equipment to be used.

Witness Lists

The Pretrial Statement should incorporate a list of witnesses you may call. Since the most common sanction for failing to list someone is their exclusion from the trial, there is a great temptation to "over list." Some courts now request that counsel identify a "plan to call" list, and a "may call" list. As you prepare this list, project the availability of the person, whether they are under the opposing party's control, whether they will require a subpoena, and if they might fight an appearance in a collateral proceeding. Beware of employees of federal or state agencies, who may resist testifying and have governmental lawyers willing to move to quash. Understand the rules on the geographic reach of your subpoenas. Negotiate with your opponent the timing of witnesses produced by the other side. If you are being intentionally disadvantaged in timing, be prepared to bring it to the court's attention. List custodians of records, with or without their name, if you are concerned that your opponent will refuse to agree to the marking of the records. List the parties on the other side in case they do not call their own clients, and broadly reserve the right to supplement. Reserve the right to call rebuttal witnesses, protecting your ability to respond when disaster or surprise strikes. In order to avoid unfair commentary about the size or nature of your witness list ("Ladies and gentlemen, Mr. Felmly says this is a simple case. It's all about a five-page contract. Well, he has listed on his witness list 35 people—35—that he intends to bring into this courtroom to explain this very simple case . . . "), use a legend on your list explaining it is to comply with the rules and is not a representation that any particular witness will be called.

Prospects for Settlement

The Pretrial Statement should reference the prospects of settlement, if required, only in very general terms. Do not set out specific offers and counter-offers unless mandated by the court, and only then in some confidential or sealed manner. Pretrial Statements are reviewed by the media and settlement is a favorite media topic in high-profile cases. If you want to encourage the court to press harder on settlement, a general statement that you continue to explore settlement or would be willing to discuss mediation may be appropriate.

Trial Counsel

In most cases, trial counsel will be known to the court from the pleadings. If someone new is being added, properly identify them and make sure they are admitted, including pro hac vice admissions for attorneys who are not from the area.

Waiver of Claims or Defenses

If you have carefully assessed and vetted your case, the Pretrial Statement is the place to describe any dropped claims. Will the defendant continue to assert comparative fault? Will certain parties be dropped as defendants? Are other third parties at fault going to be identified or waived? Is the fraud claim being dropped? All these issues should be addressed.

Admissions of liability by defendants are not uncommon at the close of discovery, even immediately before trial. What will the jury be told about the underlying facts? The defendant will seek to curtail discussion of any wrongdoing that may have caused the damages. A drunken high-speed race by the defendant driver becomes "the automobile accident" under this approach. These statements in admitted liability cases are intensely negotiated.

In any trial, the jury needs some brief orienting description by the judge as jury selection and voir dire is undertaken. I suggest you prepare that description, try to get agreement with your opponents, and either put it in the Pretrial Statement or provide it as an attachment. Similarly, or perhaps in the same statement, the description of the facts admitted for liability purposes should be prepared. Often facts relating to wrongful conduct bear on the fear, emotional distress, or severity of injuries that the plaintiff suffered. The negotiated description will provide a toned down description of events, but should generally let the jury know what really happened.

The Rest of the Pretrial Package

Depending on local rules and practices, a number of other pre-paratory documents are likely to be filed as part of the pretrial process. These are the most common in my experience.

Proposed Jury Instructions

Most courts request that counsel prepare proposed jury instructions, at least on issues that are not boilerplate. Instructions on the role of court and jury, what is and what is not evidence, burdens of proof and the like should not require a counsel submitted version. Most jurisdictions have either model instructions, or at least have established "bench book" instructions used by judges in most cases. Submitted instructions should generally follow the model forms, with variation or rewriting being clearly called out to the court and your opponent, with good reasons supporting the changes provided. There are some situations where a model instruction has not kept up with recent case law or is simply wrong. Instructions on negligence relating to "errors of judgment" or "mere errors of judgment" have provided lawyers much debate, for example. Where there is a novel question of law, or a change in existing laws, the new instruction should be carefully researched and a brief memorandum relating to that instruction is appropriate.

Avoid the temptation to cram commentary on the facts or evidence into the draft instructions, unless you know the judge prefers that style. Review your opponent's submissions carefully, examining for argument and commentary, or outright revision of a model instruction.

The Special Verdict Form

Prepare verdict forms requiring the jury to make specific factual findings and resolve multiple claims (sometimes with varying burdens of proof), as well as decide on verdicts resolving counterclaims between multiple parties. These forms require a great deal of care since the jury will navigate them when deciding your important case. Too often the preparation of the verdict form to be provided to the jury is done late in the trial, as the judge is anticipating the charge to the jury. The format, content, and extent of detail in a special verdict form present huge tactical decisions that may caution against submitting your draft during the pretrial process. However, there is no excuse for not working on it and determining the advantages or disadvantages of combining certain findings (such as breach of duty and causation versus separating such elements of the plaintiff's burden into discrete findings). At a minimum, it is prudent to have a pro forma special verdict form in your trial file with preliminary thoughts on what you will propose to the court.

In my experience, the most troublesome element in jury trials relating to personal injury is the causation finding. Based upon the requisites of proof in some jurisdictions, the jury may struggle with whether it is "more probable than not" that a particular outcome caused "or contributed to cause" the plaintiff's damages. I have had at least three trials where jurors requested a dictionary to assist in their deliberations—in each case they wanted help in defining the word "proximate" which related to the causation language in jury verdict forms or jury instructions which had produced deadlock.

Increasingly, the ability to allocate some measure of fault for a tortious event may be claimed to be borne by a third party. If your jurisdiction permits other parties at fault (not litigants in the action) to be allocated a portion of the plaintiff's damage, the handling of those persons on a verdict form is complicated. This is especially true in a case involving potentially large numbers of third parties, such other potentially responsible parties in an environmental Superfund site. Plan ahead for such issues.

Requests for Findings of Fact and Rulings of Law

In a bench trial, the court will commonly request proposed "Requests for Findings of Fact and Rulings of Law." These will, of course, require careful conformity to the evidence actually presented at trial, but many judges require these filings prior to trial, recognizing that updates and revisions will occur. There are a variety of ways to present these requests, most typically laying out the factual issues in a complaint-like fashion and then assembling the rulings of law, with appropriate legal citations. Sometimes, however, it is helpful to organize the requests by issue, combining or integrating factual paragraphs with legal rulings. In either case, the requests should be drafted with an eye to direct adoption or quotation by the judge into the decision or order. Make it easy for the judge to drop the requested finding into a narrative order. Avoid excess hyperbole and attack, and try to draft it in language that lends itself to adoption.

Motions in Limine

We arrived to draw the jury in this products liability death case an hour or so before the appointed time, carting into the courtroom the boxes of evidence and posters depicting the mechanical parts at issue. We were greeted by opposing counsel in the lobby. He handed me approximately 13 motions in limine that he had just filed with the clerk. Many of the motions were attacks on our expert witnesses. Most were asking the judge to keep out the opinions. There had been no pretrial filing or indication that a challenge to experts would be forthcoming. The court would hear the motions, the clerk advised, before the jury draw, which would be delayed for "an hour or so."

We drew the jury at about 3:00 p.m. We had spent hours on the motions, with many objections being fashioned on the fly.

Today, those motions in limine, to say nothing of a complicated *Frye/Daubert* challenge as to the qualifications or ability of an expert to express opinion testimony would be filed no later than the Pretrial Package. In addition to motions trying to limit or exclude experts on their testimony, motions in limine frequently involve subsequent remedial actions, (modifications to the defective product, fixing the broken stairs, changing the harassment reporting policy . . .), issues of insurance or other types of indemnification, questions bearing on the medical records of a party, balancing relevancy and privacy interests (prior abortions, substance abuse, etc.). The filing of a motion in limine to keep out evidence is rarely mandatory, and counsel can usually hold their fire until the matter is raised in testimony. Then, they can either timely object or approach the side bar to ask the court to preclude lines of testimony. Raising an issue before trial has benefits when you want a reasoned, researched decision. But, sometimes you want instinctive fairness and you hold the objections for trial. Rulings on motions in limine provide some certainty before the case is started as to particular controversial evidence. This can impact settlement. However, in most jurisdictions, rulings on evidence are subject to review and counsel must renew previous objections based on the pretrial ruling during the trial. It is critical that counsel not "open the door" to such evidence by unfairly getting into the excluded topics.

One of the interesting side notes to history is the fact that the Nixon Oval Office "Watergate" tapes and transcripts contained communications relating to unrelated issues. This included conversations between the President and his executive staff with the senior management of a U.S. automaker about whether the federal government would mandate airbag installations in the early 1970s. During the discovery in my case against that manufacturer claiming the deceased's car was defective, I had subpoenaed the then-CEO of the company. The judge quashed that subpoena, ruling it was too intrusive and burdensome on this industry icon. I then attempted to take and present a video deposition of one of Nixon's principal advisors who was present for Oval Office discussions of the topics.

Defendant's motion in limine sought to exclude both the deposition and the U.S. Archives certified copies of the transcripts of the discussion between the President and the company CEO. Under a finding that the risk of prejudice outweighed the probative value, and no doubt mindful that the media was extensively covering the upcoming trial, the court excluded the "Watergate" transcripts. The judge indicated that he would revisit his ruling if the defendant "opened the door."

During the third week or so of trial, the testifying defendant's engineer responded to my cross-examination on his knowledge of the airbag issue, by explaining he was involved way back in the 1970s. Indeed, he went on to explain that he went with the company's CEO to brief the President of the United States in the Oval Office. His knowledge of airbag development was long-standing and deep.

Keeping one eye on the witness, and reaching my hand back to receive from my paralegal the transcripts, the red wax seals and ribbons of the certified copies shining brightly, the jury began to wonder what was about to happen. I could hear defense counsel's chair beginning to scrape backwards as he rose for his objection. It was clear to me the judge was focused on me, anticipating my efforts to walk through the "door."

Mr. Felmly: Your Honor, should I approach the court at sidebar before proceeding—

Defense counsel: Your Honor, you have already ruled . . .

At side bar: The court immediately ruled that the door was opened by this witness, who just stumbled in. As I recall it now, the judge actually used his hand to twist the doorknob, pulling back the door, as he announced his ruling.

In a moment, the jury was transported to the Nixon Oval Office.

As this story points out, rulings on motions in limine can be instantly reversed, or evaded during the trial, once the trial judge sees how the evidence impacts the case, or the fear of possible prejudice abates. In an extreme example, multiple pretrial rulings made before trial, excluding devastating information about a professional defendant, were reversed by the trial judge on the fourth or fifth time we re-addressed the request during trial. Each time it was clear the court was torn and then, finally, changed the ruling after seeing how the opposing attorney was unfairly capitalizing on exclusion of the evidence. This reversal occurred after we had rested our case, interrupting the defendant's case. The court called a Chambers conference where the judge announced he would allow the plaintiff's case to be re-opened to call the key witness to the stand to present the prior excluded evidence. It is "never over until it's over" on such challenges and do not give up if you know the court ruling is a close call.

Weigh carefully how you will deal with motions in limine.

Requests Related to Voir Dire

For most of my years of trial practice, New Hampshire did not permit attorney-conducted voir dire, except in certain high-stakes criminal cases. The judge would provide the jury with a number of cut-and-dried questions about knowledge of the parties or bias, most often permitting counsel to provide written questions for the judge to ask or pose to the jurors who raised issues. The juror would come up to the bench and counsel and the court would discuss the issue at side bar, where some limited follow-up questions by counsel to the juror were often permitted. This is still the system generally used in our federal court and in many jurisdictions.

This system will often work reasonably well to identify problems with people called to be jurors in your case. It is greatly enhanced if you provide the court with a suggested description of the case that profiles facts that you expect will create strong feelings on the part of jurors (e.g., motorcycles, sexual harassment, ethnic or religion groups, unpopular corporate defendants). The statement you propose should be framed to recognize the probability of strong feelings in the panel and the fact that it is perfectly normal to have feelings on issues. It should also recognize, however, that the court is counting on the juror to disclose those feelings. Opening remarks by the court can advise that the existence of strong feelings will not disqualify them in all cases, and that no embarrassment or discomfort will result from identifying such bias. Some courts have this explanation to jurors down to a science, and jury selection in such courts is very natural and effective. In cases where you do not think the court will provide that talk, write it up and try to get your opponent to agree to its presentation. Present it to the court. Many judges will edit your proposal a bit, but still use the gist of it.

Assuming there will be some counsel directed voir dire, either to the panel or in follow-up at side bar after the court's questioning, prepare for it. The type of juror responses will often be predictable. If your client is well-known, some potential jurors may be familiar with them or have had corporate dealings with them. Be cognizant of the fact that some jurors may have had medical events, accidents, employment disputes, or other types of factual events that may be present in your case. Think about how to elicit more information without offending the potential juror with invasion of their privacy. Prepare and present open-ended questions and practice asking them. "How many of you folks have experienced. . . ?" Get a show of hands, and follow up. As to highly charged ideological issues ("too many lawsuits," malpractice claims "driving up" health costs, drunk driving, and sexual harassment, for example), rehearse your questions carefully, stressing the normalcy of all of us having strong feelings or past experiences on certain issues.

Jury voir dire and selection is not about picking a "great jury" or folks uniquely predisposed to the position of your client. It is about eliminating the people who have adverse bias or traits that make them a bad potential juror for your case. Intelligence, integrity, willingness to serve, open-mindedness, fairness, even humor are all in play, but in the end you have a small number of preemptory challenges to eliminate the people who worry you the most. Set up for this process in the Pretrial Package by requesting how you want the court to conduct jury selection.

Establishing the Trial Schedule

If your jurisdiction provides substantial advance notice for the trial of the case, you will have already advised clients and key witnesses to hold the trial period. It is now critical that you contact those witnesses and begin to shape the actual schedule of testimony. Many lawyers practice in courts where the trial notice comes within a month, even a week or two before the trial. In such settings, anticipating that timing, remaining aware of medical or travel conflicts of your witnesses, and trying to coordinate with the clerk's office and your opponents to avoid impossible scheduling is all time well spent. While it all depends on your local practice, extraordinary scheduling concerns should be anticipated and communicated, perhaps in a letter to the court. I have experienced the systems where there is no concern for your schedule, other trials, or the demands on your witness. If that is your lot, you just have to hang on.

Expert witness scheduling presents the most severe demands and problems. First, the experts are often expensive and sending off $15,000 of prepaid expert fees for a full day of in-court testimony demands we schedule the day reliably. Second, the timing of expert testimony may demand laying the factual foundation for the opinion testimony. How many days of fact witnesses will precede your expert taking the stand? Is your expert's testimony dependent on other experts testifying first—should the surgeon testify prior to the pathologist who will describe the nature of the malignancy and statistical probability of a cure? You will encounter many situations where expert scheduling will preclude the perfect sequencing of witness testimony. I once was forced to commence a plaintiff's medical negligence case by calling my key expert as the first witness. He was flying out of the country at 7:00 p.m. that evening and could not be available at any other day in the trial. You can adapt to these crises and witnesses can be called "out of order," even in your opponent's case, but prioritize your efforts at scheduling as early as possible.

Your client's schedule demands special attention. If you represent a corporate party, who will serve as the client representative? Is house counsel the best individual to personify the company at counsel table for a three-week trial? Is there a key businessperson who will testify, have a credible stake in the outcome, and who makes an excellent impression? Is that person available for what may become a good part of the month of November? Does your plaintiff work for a living in a job that may not permit a three-week leave of absence? All these issues, which at one time you reassured the client/witness were bridges you would "cross when we come to them," are now here.

At this point, you should be drafting a detailed chart actually laying out the trial schedule in time blocks. You need to decide how you will prioritize—whether with a strong initial witness, or perhaps using a chronological theme starting with some incident eyewitness, police, or other first responder. Should you start with the injured client, stressing strong liability, great personality, and horrible damages? There is no proven formula for such scheduling, but you must work with your team and the schedules of witnesses to establish the plan. You should lock in your experts or those witnesses with inflexible schedules. Key experts with inflexible schedules *must* get on and off the stand on the day chosen. Start them first thing in the morning, even if it means getting court permission to interrupt a witness who carried over from the previous day. Work out as best as you can an estimate of the required time for your expert's direct and make sure you provide your opponent a comparable and fair time for cross. Some opponents with limited trial experience will play games with their estimate, first because they know it will require you to rush your witness examination, and also because they hope their prolonged cross will eliminate any clean-up redirect with your expert at day's end. Plan for all of this, and if you are in that box, alert the judge of this planned witness schedule at the end of the previous day's testimony, even asking for some flexibility on extending the trial day for 20 minutes if it turns out your opponent's cross exam takes the entire afternoon session. This communication will generally get your expert to his or her airplane on time.

Charting out the schedule for more routine or flexible witnesses should presume that the trial day gets shortened a bit by delays which are inherent in trial scheduling (motions lists, jurors who are late, "The Chief Judge called me in chambers on an administrative matter just as I was about to enter the courtroom . . . 'I am going to tell the jury to return a few minutes later than usual, say 2:00 p.m., because I am alone here today and there is a very short motion for ex parte relief I need to handle at 1:30 p.m. . . .'").

As a result, I tend to plan the schedule chart as follows:

- Jury selection and opening statements will consume at least a half day. If there is a view and pre-view statement, it is unlikely a witness will be called on day 1.
- A substantial key witness should be charted for a full half day.
- A key expert with scheduling inflexibility should get a full day on the schedule. You need to have other witnesses with flexibility available to fill the rest of the day, but plan for the worst and make sure the key expert gets off that day.
- Routine witnesses should be given an hour. Three can usually be done in a morning or afternoon session. Sometimes

the themes and storytelling demand they be presented in sequence.

- The playing of videotape depositions or reading of transcribed depositions of unavailable witnesses often provides some flexibility in trial where parties "run out of witnesses." This requires the video depositions to be formatted in a manner that permits quick deployment.

These rules of thumb apply to estimating your opponent's case as well. I always endeavor to establish an understanding that the proposed or planned schedule should be open for discussion with opposing counsel. If they balk about this, I go to the judge to get some insistence on mutual cooperation. Many judges now expect counsel to provide a detailed written schedule for the trial, recognizing that it requires constant updating and adjustment. Many trial days end with a brief preview by counsel to the court on the day ahead. Try to establish that process if the court does not.

I know trial lawyers that regard such efforts at scheduling as overdone, claiming it is impossible due to the many contingencies and uncertainties in play. I have butted heads with such adversaries, and usually they come around and cooperate more fully when they realize that the judge and jury appreciate it.

Prepare a Draft of Your Opening Statement

Perhaps the most concrete and valuable recommendation in this handbook is that you prepare a solid outline for your Opening Statement in the period 30 to 20 days from trial. Most often, trial lawyers still prepare the Opening after everything else is done and the case is about to start. The final weekend push has the associate and paralegal packing exhibit boxes and assembling the equipment and paperwork of trial, while the lead attorney is sequestered in a conference room down the hall trying to capture the themes, imagery, and persuasive elements that will comprise the Opening Statement. Defense counsel may have so much trial experience that she will have a group of fairly stock Opening points at her fingertips regarding burden of proof, keeping an "open mind" until all the evidence is in, and the like. The rest of such a defendant's Opening may be assembled on the fly—drawing off and rebutting the plaintiff lawyer's Opening.

In truth, capturing thoughts for your Opening should have been an ongoing process during the entire case. Jot down your first impressions of your client, particularly poignant comments by eyewitnesses and analogies drawing the evidence that come to you on the long ride to your weekend cabin. All of these thoughts should be captured in electronic note-taking or written subfile entries. Now is the time to dig them all out and consider them for inclusion.

Irrespective of whether you bring that level of energy to anticipation of the Opening, waiting until the last weekend or relying on stock or rote repetition of prior Openings is simply a mistake. Here are the key benefits of preparing your Opening in outline form prior to attending the pretrial conference with the court and your opponent:

- It will force you to assess and choose key themes for the trial. It is time to fish or cut bait. Drafting the Opening illuminates the case, the problems, and the wishful thinking with an intense beam.
- Evidentiary problems, gaps in foundation, and glaring hearsay will all become real as you envision yourself telling court and jury what the evidence will show.

"Your Honor, I do not want to interrupt counsel, but I must note an objection to Mr. Felmly telling the jury that the evidence will show that Mrs. Price, the decedent, made any statement prior to the collision. As the court knows, this is plainly impermissible hearsay. . . "

There may be several ways to get Mrs. Price's pre-impact statement into evidence, depending on the local hearsay rules of deceased persons, or excited utterances, and this is time to prepare for those battles.

- Outlining your Opening Statement will empower you. The reason we prefer to put off drafting the Opening until the Final Weekend is not because we forgot—it is just hard work. Drafting the Opening, even as an outline, requires marshaling the facts, deciding on a sequence of delivery, weighing the themes, deciding how to handle weaknesses in the case, and considering what exhibits to employ in the Opening. All direct how you are going to tell this story. Once you have done it, even if it will be expanded and refined dozens of times before trial, its existence provides confidence—the reality that the case will come together, and that you will be ready to present it.
- Having an outline or a draft is a useful fact to mention at the pretrial conference.

"Your Honor, just one other thing, working and trying to tune up my Opening I think will require a little more time than the 30 minutes under the Rule. I know I will not go longer than 40 to 45 minutes and hope that you will be agreeable to that time frame."

It is just helpful in a lot of ways to have your opponent assuming you are fairly well set on your opening 20 days out from trial.

Chapter 4

Day 20 to Day 10

Final Pretrial Conference

The trial court will generally provide or require a conference two weeks to ten days before the scheduled trial to resolve motions, consider whether settlement is possible, and discuss a wide range of housekeeping issues. In my experience, judges who employ this type of trial management conference are better prepared for the issues about to confront the court, make better rulings on motions in limine, and generally provide a better professional experience for all involved. I have experienced the alternatives where preparation is seen to be too time-consuming, unnecessary, or "that's not the way we do it here, Mr. Felmly." Counsel should be proactive in approaching the conference, often preparing an actual written agenda, which you should provide, if the court would appreciate it. There is a line between helpful preparation and usurpation of the judge's leadership at the conference, and it is imperative that you not cross that line. Give a copy of the agenda to your opponent prior to going into chambers, making it something both counsel are engaged in offering.

The topics discussed in the preceding chapter on preparing pretrial filings will now provide much of the information that will dominate the pretrial conference. Be prepared for motions in limine to be argued, assuming that timely objections have been filed. This may require you to request a record of the pre-trial conference, if one is not routinely provided. In the Day, such conferences were almost always held in chambers, often without a record. Argument on motions might be taken into open court, following the more general discussion of housekeeping matters. Today, the conference will often be on the record, in open court. Just be careful that you protect the record on issues that demand one.

The court will likely ask for some status report on settlement. You should have your response prepared. If you want the court to press for an eighth-inning mediation, this is the time you may want to suggest that possibility. This should be done without any suggestion that the trial would be delayed. Many courts require that client representatives with settlement authority attend, or be available by phone to participate in the pretrial conference. This is especially so if the conference will address settlement. I recall a final pretrial conference in federal court that began in the late afternoon and ended at about 11:00 p.m. The trial judge conducted a cross-country telephone negotiation over many hours with insurance carrier senior claims representatives on the West Coast. Ultimately, the judge hammered out a settlement at the pretrial conference. More often, client representatives wait in the court lobby or at the end of a phone that does not ring, but be sure you have them prepared for settlement discussions that may arise.

I have suggested using the conference to address housekeeping and trial procedural issues. Here is a list that may be of help—

- Confirm the date the trial will start. Are there any prior cases before yours? If there are, do your best to nail down your starting date.
- Confirm the details of the trial day. Tactfully determine if the judge must deal with other matters before the trial

starts each day. If so, cancel your post-trial vacation. This is going to take a long time. Get a sense of the practice as to the noon break, and at what time the trial day will end in the afternoon. Will there be any flexibility if we need to go ten or fifteen extra minutes at the end of a day in order to finish a witness? This is harder to achieve in these times of court austerity.

- Will there be counsel-conducted voir dire? Discuss all of the voir dire issues. Will there be time expectations set with regard to any counsel-directed voir dire?
- Will the jury be allowed to take notes? How will that be handled?
- Will the jurors be allowed to ask questions of witnesses? More and more courts permit this practice. How will the questions be vetted and reviewed by the judge? Will the questions be presented to the witness by the judge for a response? Will counsel be provided opportunity for further questions after the juror's question is answered in order to clarify or clean up after the witness has responded?
- Electronic presentation aids: What does the court have for equipment? Is it available? Who is the coordinator? When can we arrange a convenient time to meet with that person and test our systems? Determine if there are any special rules on having or using cell phones in the building. Many courts have special procedures or prohibitions, some resembling the systems of the Old West where pistols of cowboys were checked at the saloon door. Can the client have a cell phone or a smart phone with e-mail? What about jurors and smart phones? What instructions will the court provide jurors on using Google Earth to investigate the accident scene, sending e-mail messages to each other, or doing their own medical or criminal records research? Statistical studies have suggested that a very high rate of jury use of the Internet is conducted, irrespective of instructions they get from the court. More and more courts are developing very

detailed juror instructions regarding the use of social media and computer research.

- Jury instructions and special verdict forms. Each of these involves not only preparation issues, but often tactical questions on when to raise particular topics. A key instruction such as that on "superseding intervening cause" may require development of evidence prior to supplying a supplemental draft instruction to the court. Think through all of this.

- Use of the facilities. Can we get into the courtroom at 8:15 a.m. every day to set up? Can we have reserved conference rooms for each side to use during the week of trial? Can we leave our boxes, equipment, and materials in the courtroom overnight? If there are early morning hearings or other uses of the courtroom before trial starts, what do you want us to do with our materials?

- If you are trying a case away, the final pretrial conference is a time to consider and display the role that your local counsel in that jurisdiction will play in the case. The court will usually want visible and material participation by the local member of the Bar. Hopefully your colleague from that jurisdiction is skilled and a valuable asset to the trial team. Make her an important part of the team. In some cases, particularly in bench trials, the court may exclude as unnecessary participation by the local member of the Bar. Be careful in accepting that offer to excuse local counsel if you believe that your colleague is well-known and respected by the trial judge.

- Use of depositions. By this point, you should have sorted out the availability of witnesses and identified what depositions will actually be read in the trial or shown to the jury on video. The court will encourage significant editing of the testimony and require parties to meet and confer on the edits. Work with opposing counsel on objections—most should be waived, and those requiring a ruling should result in a plan to present them to the court with enough time to obtain a ruling. As noted earlier, make every effort to have your video depositions in a synchronized digital format for ease in managing edits.

- Sequestration of witnesses. Be sure you understand the local rules and practice of having witnesses in the courtroom during the testimony of other witnesses. Civil cases in New Hampshire are very relaxed on such matters, while in trials elsewhere I have encountered very strict rules on courtroom presence of witnesses or communication with witnesses by anyone regarding the testimony that has occurred in court. Make sure you understand and follow such rules religiously.

- Discuss the mechanics of jury selection with the court. Huge variety exists in jury selection procedures, often within the same jurisdiction. When does the court conduct voir dire of the jurors? Is it panel voir dire in open court—at least initially? Will jurors be responding at side bar or in open court? How many preemptory challenges does each side get—the rule or statute provides a number, but if one side, say the defendants, involves three parties, do they get the specified number times three, while the plaintiff gets one-third as many? Most judges end up working with counsel under the practical circumstances of the case to pick a fair number for each "group." Will the replacement juror for a "struck juror" be from a pre-picked queue (the "struck method")? Or will the clerk pick a new name from the shoebox? Jury selection using the struck method enables counsel to assess the replacements in a more sensible and ordered way.

- Plan how to manage challenges for cause and discuss this with the court. Challenges for cause can come in several places in the jury selection process. First, the qualifying question from the judges to the panel may elicit relationships or bias that immediately leads to disqualification or challenge. More commonly, the responses of panel members during the voir dire process elicits bias which becomes a basis for challenge. Managing such a process and keeping the discussion private is difficult. In some circumstances handling for cause challenges in chambers is preferable.

Jury selection is a hectic, fast-paced event. Everyone is watching, especially jurors who wonder what you were thinking when you strike them. You need to have a system to identify the called juror and measure them against your prior assessment or research as to that juror. However, the juror questionnaires or comments of people who know the juror do not replace your immediate face-to-face reaction to the person. Do not be a slave to your chart. You need to stay calm, communicate discreetly with your team, avoid telegraphing dismay or elation to your opponent, and observe the qualities of this juror as they enter the jury box. Also remember how many preemptory challenges you have left. Make sure you know how alternates are handled for selection in your court. Is there pressure to allow all of them to join the jury and sit in on deliberations, ending up in a fourteen-person jury? In general, try to avoid that, since it maximizes the potential for a hung jury. If the alternates are selected just before the case goes to the jury, you must assume that your preemptories will be exercised against the entire array, including alternates. How will the jury foreperson be chosen? If you are drawing juries under a struck system, you need to always know what the panel consists of as each choice is made so that you do not waste a preemptory against a person in the array who can never be reached in light of the number of preemptories. I realize this all sounds confusing and may have lots of variations in your jurisdiction. But do not be embarrassed to ask for clarification as you start the process and make sure you know how it's going to be conducted.

Marking Exhibits and Resolving Objections

Courts utilizing the pretrial procedures described in this handbook commonly require the parties to identify the exhibits to be marked at trial and provide a procedure for counsel to identify and attempt to resolve objections. The nature of the procedures, the meet and confer process, and the filings made with the court to accomplish this process are often quite diverse. In general, parties will identify and provide characterization of the nature of objections. The common objections of relevance, lack of foundation, hearsay, and privilege are frequently set forth. If you think the court will rule on objections based simply on this description, a more detailed argument supporting the objection will be required. Most often courts will also require that counsel meet and confer regarding the objections. This process usually works well, with give and take occurring on similar objections and traded off. As this negotiation moves forward, there is usually some designation made for exhibits that are subject to objection, often that exhibit is marked "for ID."

It is helpful in preparing the exhibit list with large numbers of documents not only to list the exhibit with a numerical or alphabetical reference (e.g. Plaintiff Exhibit 1; Defendant Exhibit A), but also to reference any discovery tracking Bates number, as well as the exhibit number of the document if it was marked during a deposition. All these aids provide information helpful to identify and track the document down in the word searchable electronic database. In some courts, the practice with respect to marking exhibits requires the plaintiff's exhibits to be marked with Arabic numerals and the defendant's to be marked with letters. In cases with large number of documents, you can end up with exhibits with markings, such as defendant's exhibit AAAAA. This process never works once the trial begins and you need to explain to the court that the large number of exhibits mandate an Arabic number designation for defense exhibits as well.

When working with a large number of documents in a series, such as 35 photos of an accident scene, it is useful to mark them as a series. The photos would be marked "Plaintiff's Exhibit 4(A), (B), (C), and so on."

Many exhibits benefit from a summary or compilation sheet accompanying voluminous records, such as medical bills, invoices in a construction dispute, and large numbers of corporate board of directors minutes. Become familiar with Federal Rule of Evidence 1006, and its corresponding state evidence rule in your jurisdiction dealing with the use of summaries, charts, and calculations, to prove the content of voluminous writings, recordings, or photographs. In cases where you are trying to prove patterns of behavior or courses of dealing drawn from many individual transactions, you may want to have a summary profile of your client's activities or treatment and its cost. A chart or summary assembling key facts from those voluminous documents is very helpful and an efficient exhibit.

Be sure you understand the court's practice with respect to documents to be used at trial only for impeachment or cross-examination. Most courts do not require prior identification or listing of such materials, preserving at least a remnant of dramatic potential for the witness to be confronted with them at cross-examination. But I have also tried with judges that required every impeaching document, article, treatise, or whatever to be disclosed, listed, and exchanged. I regard that to be impractical, inefficient, and a practice that serves to diminish the truth-finding process. In any case, you need to be sure you know the rules with respect to impeachment and cross-examination exhibits. Also be very alert for statutes or rules that may require particular types of documents be disclosed or noticed prior to their use. The use of prior criminal records or other sensitive materials often are subject to special notification statutes or rules.

Handling highly confidential information may require a wide array of special procedures, instructions, labeling, or packaging with respect to exhibits. This is of special concern in intellectual property cases where formulas, customer lists, sensitive financial or business information, or true trade secrets need to be protected. In general, there will already be a Protective Order in place that should define and describe the practices to be followed in managing and safeguarding such confidential information. In cases involving sensitive, or potentially sensational or inflammatory photos or exhibits (nudity, injury photos, etc.), package and maintain these materials with great sensitivity. If such confidential or sensitive material is being marked as an exhibit, special labeling and legends will be required.

Oversize, and even gigantic exhibits, such as models, exemplars of equipment, or vehicles, all require planning and careful coordination with the courthouse staff. The judge will also expect you to make arrangements for the storage of such equipment immediately after trial if an appeal is filed.

Preparing the Client for Trial

Most clients have limited experience and understanding of the trial process and dynamics. While an experienced insurance claims representative or corporate in-house litigation counsel will not require much education or communication in order to prepare them for this major event in the case, you will be well served orienting your business clients and personal injury plaintiffs and defendants to the demanding and stressful process they are about to experience.

I find it useful to schedule a personal meeting with the client representatives at a time approximating the final pretrial conference. These individuals are likely not just your client contacts, but usually have some role as witnesses in the case. They will also be the key individuals involved in any settlement decision appropriate to this pretrial period. While settlement and preparing for testimony are elements of this meeting, they are not the principal focus. This is more a process to dispel the fears, convey confidence in the nature of case preparation, and educate the client about the upcoming courthouse experience and trial process.

Of course, the nature of these meetings can vary greatly with the sophistication and experience of the client, and certainly some clients such as the elderly, young persons, or individuals with cognitive impairments demand much greater attention. I have had the experience of representing at trial several individuals with severe mental and cognitive impairments. Such circumstances impose very heavy burdens on trial counsel and generally require a trusted and able family member or friend to work along with you to accompany the client during the trial. If the impairments require adaptation or modification of the courtroom facilities for seating, audio, or visual problems, you should have worked this out by now with the courthouse personnel, and reassured the client that those needs would be respected. Here are a variety of issues you will likely want to discuss with the client in anticipation of the trial.

- **Report on scheduling and courthouse facilities.** Alert the client regarding the status of any final hearings and the date of the jury draw. If the jury draw will not immediately precede commencement of the case, explain to the client that they need to be present for the draw. Explain the probable commencement date for the trial, the daily timing of the trial day, and when you want them present in the courthouse for each trial day. Explain you will orient them to the building before the trial starts, but discuss parking, directions to the courthouse, and access through security in anticipation of their arrival on the first day. If you have concerns with either firearms or other problems that arise with security, deal with them now. I was awaiting screening in a county courthouse line when an accompanying out-of-state lawyer asked me quietly if the bailiffs would hold his handgun during our proceedings that morning. We went back and left it in the car. You cannot make this stuff up.

- **Tactfully educate the client about the importance of time-liness and attendance throughout the trial.** No exceptions. They must be on time. Discuss how to notify you in the event of any emergency in their attendance—if you wait to do this, such problems will arise, often generating great stress.

> *I recall the call at 5:00 a.m. from my client who was sobbing and trying to explain that her sister, who was eight months pregnant, had miscarried during the middle of the night and that the family was in turmoil. That sister was the witness on the stand at 4:30 p.m. the preceding day, testifying as a damage witness on behalf of my client, when the trial recessed for the day. How would we deal with her testimony or suspension of it, with the jury and with the judge? A series of very early morning calls to the clerk of court and opposing counsel ultimately resolved that the witness would not go back on the stand and the jury was advised that the parties had simply decided to forgo the necessity of bringing her back. It took at least a year off my life.*

- **Orient the client as to their role at trial.** Clients always want to know what to wear to court. Your response should vary with the client and the case, but discuss your expectations. Trials do not always require the men to wear a tie and sport coat, but respectful, appropriate attire and grooming is important. Beware of logos, ideological lapel pins (American flags are fine), and exposed tattoos. What would you wear to church or an important town event?
- **Explain to the client the visibility they will have, not just in the courtroom, but in any venue where the jury will come**

into contact with them. This is, of course, much more likely in smaller rural courthouses where contacts during the noon hour, in the parking lot, and in other common areas can be expected. Please smile, be polite, offer a simple greeting, perhaps a comment on the ongoing rainstorm, but that's it. If they race to park in the last remaining space in the courthouse parking lot, they can be sure that luck will always have it that the other car they push out of the spot will be driven by one of our jurors. Be immensely courteous and respectful of everyone. Speaking of cars, advise the client to avoid any logos or decals on the car that are likely to insult or worry any significant percentage of the jury. Decals about how your child is an honor student at the local school are fine, pronouncements on the Second Amendment, the legalization of marijuana, or Confederate battle flags raise different issues. And leave the Ferrari at home.

- **Caution the client about conversations in the courthouse lobby, lunchroom, or interactions with witnesses in a manner that may raise jurors' concerns.** There are no secrets in a courthouse.

I have had several experiences where jurors raised concerns to the trial judge regarding the interaction of witnesses with parties. I recall a juror who saw the doctor defendant in a medical negligence case hugging a key nurse witness in the parking lot during the noon recess. Who would have thought . . . ? The juror told the bailiff, and a chambers conference with counsel, the court, and the juror ensued. It was quite a discussion.

I work hard with clients to try to enhance their respect of the role and service of the jury. I also explain that I have served on a jury and have first-hand understanding that jurors (1) miss nothing that occurs in a courthouse involving the parties. (Every smirk, every passed note, any tension between lawyer and client is noted by somebody on the panel.); and (2) since they are told not to discuss the issues in the case, they constantly talk about the people in the case. They try to figure out who the spectators sitting in the back are ("is that the insurance adjuster?") and they very carefully assess related family members and relationships. Clients need to understand these dynamics and be carefully educated about their visibility, without going so far as to terrify them about the intrusiveness of the jury's observations.

- Make sure the client is aware of courthouse demeanor. Determine and deal with whether cell phone and smart phone use in the courthouse is permissible. Even in courthouses that permit parties or counsel to use their phones, they should be instructed as to how to avoid any interruption as telephone calls are received. Discuss permissible note taking and note sharing by the client with counsel or with other parties. Moderate passage of notes from client to lawyer is fine, showing engagement in the case and interest. Eating food, gum chewing, and unwrapping crinkly, loud candy wrappers, even in a sport coat pocket, are a problem. Explain the importance of side bar conferences and instruct the client to sit quietly while they occur. Remind them to be attentive to their body position and their feet. I once had a juror, months after a trial when it was permissible to discuss the jurors' impressions of the case, helpfully explain to me that I would be quicker rising with objections if I kept my loafers on my feet during my opposing counsel's examination. I do better with my shoes on now. Jurors miss nothing.

- **Case status, settlement, and case problems.** Provide at this orientation a sense of the schedule you are following and advise when you will be meeting with witnesses in order to prepare their testimony. This is not that meeting, but it may be appropriate to suggest certain things they can do in order to orient themselves to being a witness. Have them review their deposition and interrogatory responses. Suggest that they drive to the scene of the event and familiarize themselves again with the layout, or review detailed records with which they need to be familiar. Provide them a high level of confidence that you will be preparing them for their testimony. Explain that such preparation will also include some role-playing and specific techniques on how to be a better witness. Also, update them on the problems and challenges of the case. Explain how you are working to resolve difficulties with the case, but provide them information they need to know that may bear on the prospects of settlement.

Chapter 5

Day 10 to Day 3

Prepare for Jury Selection

In many courts there is a system of obtaining juror question-naires that describe certain biographical information on each juror. These questionnaires vary in content and detail from jurisdiction to jurisdiction, but represent your key resource on the characteristics of your jury panel. Increased concerns with personal privacy have changed the way in which these questionnaires are managed, and to some degree have limited the content about family circumstances. Generally, the ques-tionnaire will identify address, occupation, some information on family status, any impairment that may impact jury service or require accommodation, and sometimes levels of educa-tion, homeownership status, and prior participation as a juror or litigant. Responding jurors generally get these completed questionnaires back to the court clerk within two weeks of a jury trial, but non-compliance is common. Some will likely be trickling in even as late as the day of trial. Always check for new questionnaires.

Determine the court procedure on access to the juror ques-tionnaires and obtain that booklet or folder of complete questionnaires as soon as it is available. You will generally be required to return the actual questionnaires after the jury draw, and there will commonly be confidentiality limitations on circulation or distribution of the questionnaires. Obtain the list of jurors, which usually provides some geographic indicator, such as a town or city, and circulate it in a circumspect way to obtain information on the panel. I find it useful to provide the list to my client; I circulate it to all staff or lawyers in the office, and commonly e-mail it to lawyer colleagues in the county or city where the trial is occurring. Make it clear in dealing with neighboring lawyers that you are not seeking any attorney-client information regarding the jurors. Of course, sometimes there are questions regarding whether a particular name on the list is indeed the individual that you will have on your jury, but you will be able to sort out these issues and any confusion. I provide a brief description of the case and identification of our client ("We are drawing a jury next Monday in Carroll County in an automobile accident case. We represent Mary Smith, who was seriously injured when a Jones Plumbing Company truck operated by Bill Jones went through a stop sign and struck Mary's car"). In my experience, all of these efforts are productive in producing helpful, sometimes vital information, about the prospective panel.

It is also important that you access the Internet to try to obtain information on jurors. This requires careful attention and instruction to your team to be sure there is no violation of court rule or jury privacy, or any actual effort to have contact with the prospective juror. Social media now comes in so many forms that any effort to describe it will likely be obsolete tomorrow; however, use of a search engine such as Google will commonly provide information on jurors and identify family data, employment and educational accomplishments, and political and community involvement. Jurors who would likely be potential juror leaders, or pose concerns in terms of their affiliations, strong views, or reliability, will frequently show up as a result of an Internet search. Of course, the importance of this will vary with the nature and notoriety of the case, but there is no substitute for obtaining information that suggests possible juror knowledge of the core issues, parties, or a particular mindset that may impact their impartiality.

You should be particularly careful with respect to social media tools, such as LinkedIn™, where the subject of the search may be able to identify that someone is searching them—from your law firm. This is not only potentially very embarrassing, but will likely violate rules prohibiting jury contact and may result in professional conduct complaints. There is an enormous amount of current commentary and developing case law on the use of social media and other Internet resources in connection with juries, and you may wish to review this to provide further information. For my purposes, the Internet provides a valuable tool, but do not undertake any intrusion into private sites or other searches which you would not be completely comfortable describing to your trial judge. One final point: in this day and age, jurors are just as likely to be conducting their own research on the Internet regarding their upcoming service as a juror. You should assume, irrespective of any instruction that the courts may give to the jury to refrain from doing research or communicating on line regarding the case, that they are likely checking out counsel in the case, your law firm, and your client. Make sure you and your client are not making public Facebook posts describing the trial process or the case. There have been cases where parties to litigation have made posts on their personal blogs describing the frailties of the trial judge and the members of the jury. It's hard to survive such craziness in trial.

In major cases with high stakes, it is not uncommon for one side or the other to use a jury consultant. These folks, not surprisingly, vary enormously in talent, cost, and usefulness. I have some, but not extensive experience, in their use, and bring a healthy skepticism to the practice. At its worst, such consultants often stress ethnic, occupational, or gender-based qualifications which are gross oversimplifications. At best, they can bring the experiences of hundreds of cases with keen insight based on the appearances and observations of the members of the community involved in the jury draw. Their usefulness will often be driven by the amount of information obtained beyond the court questionnaires. In some major cases, the parties on both sides may be able to convince the court to issue to the jury a more detailed, case-specific questionnaire. Such a tool dramatically enhances the data regarding the jury demographics and the ability of a consultant to add value to the selection process. The ability to gain maximum value from a consultant requires the ability to communicate with her in real time during the actual draw and the exercise of preemptory challenges. These issues arise in fairly rare and specialized cases, and how to handle such consultant or team communications in the public forum of a trial requires careful consideration with the court, and likely some explanation to the jury from the judge to ensure jurors are comfortable with the process. In the end, all this jury research and planning will "sugar off" (as they say in maple syrup production) to decisions on how to exercise three to five preemptory challenges to get rid of the jurors you think will be awful on your panel.

Preparing Your Witnesses

The Direct and Cross-Examination Outlines

Witness preparation requires creation of outlines for their examination, as well as meetings with each witness to prepare them for the process of testifying. Most folks do not have experience as witnesses and it is a learned skill. At this point you should have a good idea about what evidence you will be able to present, and what topics or exhibits the court will likely allow and/or exclude. The extent of direct preparation you can accomplish depends greatly on your relationship with the witness. Your client, family, friends, and experts are all available to you within the limitation of their schedules and the preparation of those people should be thorough. Key witnesses in major cases will require multiple preparation sessions, often spread out over several weeks. Police officers, other governmental investigators, and responders may be largely unavailable or too busy to provide you with the time to prepare. Many such witnesses are prepared in a 10-minute phone call or on the courthouse steps when they respond to your subpoena to appear. Your preparation must adapt to circumstances, but you should be planning now for how to achieve their preparation to the best extent possible.

The preparation of a solid witness outline demands a plan in place as to the order in which the witness will testify. What evidence is already before the jury when this witness appears? A lead-off or broad introductory witness demands the greatest effort and care in preparation. You will need to determine how to lead off—are there topics or impacts you need to address before dealing with the events or incident in a chronological way?

> *"Mary, before we talk with the jury about the accident and what happened that day, we are all very mindful that you are here in this courthouse in a wheelchair. I would like to first have you describe to the jury the injuries you experienced in the crash and the impairments and impacts those injuries have had and continue to have on your life. So, if it's okay with you, can you first tell us how you were injured, the nature of those injuries, and what parts of your body were affected and are now impaired by the injuries received in the crash. . . ?"*

You will be constantly balancing the advantages of primacy—dealing with important things first—versus circumstances where you build to an important finish. One size certainly does not fit all in terms of presenting evidence. The preparation of your witness outline and seeing it in the context of the outlines of other witnesses will assist in how you make these choices and whether your projected order of witnesses will require change.

You will also be forced to decide how to deal with difficult or damaging aspects of the case. You will likely have already begun that assessment in the dealing with the drafting of your Opening Statement. How will you deal with facts that are harmful? Comparative fault, lapses in judgment or truthfulness in statements made by the client/witness, and similar problems are common and you will need to decide whether to hit them head on or prepare your witness to respond to them when raised by your opponent on cross.

The witness outline is not a script. It does not mandate particular phrasing, except in the case of evidence that must meet precise technical standards. Perhaps the best example of such an area of testimony is that seeking of the ultimate opinion from an expert in a professional negligence case—

> *"Dr. White, do you have an opinion based upon your training, education, and experience as a surgeon over thirty years, (pause) and your careful review of the medical records of the plaintiff, Mary Smith, (pause) and your understanding and knowledge of the accepted standards of surgical care appropriate to the circumstances of Mary Smith's treatment and surgery, (pause) and applying and based upon a standard of medical probability [or reasonable medical certainty if your jurisdiction demands that description], whether the surgical care provided by the defendant, Dr. Johnson, was in accordance with or met those accepted standards of care or practice?"*

Some of you could improve on this question. Indeed, it is a mouthful. Short pauses between key points help. Some would integrate causation of injury; I would prefer to cover causation in a second follow-up question, which I would generally also write out. The point is, there will be questions that raise specific standards of proof in your jurisdiction, often dealing with "medical probability," "reasonable medical certainty," "accepted standards of care," and if your opponent and your judge do not hear those words, the objection light goes on. There is room for liturgy in communication. Some of these questions are useful to write out.

Most of your outline will be key words and phrases that will permit you to recall and progress through the examination. Exhibit references will be integrated into the outline and prominently noted, usually in red. A separate list of exhibits to be used or shown to the witness and displayed on the presentation monitor is kept, and provided to your presentation operator, so that person can bring them up in sequence. Each of those listed exhibits will be put into an ordered folder in the presentation software, and any highlighting, split imaging, or other modification or enhancement of the exhibit is noted and planned. If the presentation of the exhibits will be through hard copy, with display in hand to the witness on the stand, or by use of Elmo projection, those exhibits must be assembled, stacked in order, and ready to go as the witness takes the stand. There is no excuse for counsel examining a witness to be rooting through the entire box of exhibits trying to find Plaintiff Exhibit 157 during the examination.

At best, the witness outline integrates a map or direction for the journey counsel will take with the witness. It will provide sequencing for introducing or using exhibits. If objections are expected on particular topics, it will contain deposition references, even case citations, evidence rules, and quotes, to argue evidentiary points. If the witness is going to be asked to leave the witness box to demonstrate or draw a diagram, the outline will have a depiction of the key points you want to show on the diagram. It will also contain stage direction on when to approach side bar to raise points that require judicial involvement—

Mr. Felmly: May I approach?
Judge: Yes, of course, counsel approach . . .

Mr. Felmly: Your Honor, as we discussed in chambers yesterday, at this point in Ms. Smith's examination, I intend to elicit testimony regarding her understanding of the permanent nature of her spinal injury. Her medical records are now marked as a full exhibit and reflect what her doctors told her. She will describe that she has been told there is no further surgery at this time that can restore her ability to walk. She is 50 years old and will, absent a true miracle, be in this wheelchair for her entire life. Dr. Hagan's testimony has described the injury to her spinal cord in detail. You asked that I approach before inquiring of her understanding, and I request I now be permitted to elicit this testimony at this time. The testimony is certainly not speculative, as opposing counsel suggested yesterday, and is grounded directly on her medical treatment and the opinions of her doctors. It is not hearsay as it is directly drawn from her medical diagnosis and treatment . . .

The preparation of witness outlines is not limited to your clients or the witnesses favorable to your side of the case. You will also prepare examinations for the direct exam you will conduct of any adverse witness or opposing parties that you intend to call in your case. These are, of course, functional cross-examination outlines, and come with the goal and challenge of not opening the door for such a witness to damage your case. Damage will arise if you do not have at your command or control the evidence and points to refute any effort at evasion, contradiction, or surprise. Your ability to achieve that control will, of course, rest on the effectiveness and thoroughness of your discovery and preparation. Mastery of the facts, records, technical literature, and the disciplines involved in the case is a start. You should predict where the witness will seek to undermine or damage your case, and have the treatises, articles, medical records, or police report references all ready to go. They should be noted in your outline. As you prepare the outline for the adverse witness, you will not only select the exhibits to be utilized or displayed on the monitors, but you will also prepare and organize for the presentation each impeachment exhibit, or deposition reference, that you predict the control of the witness might require. You should know how the witness will attempt to evade, and instantly be prepared to display the impeaching reference.

Key deposition testimony is significant to this impeachment process. The outline should annotate virtually every topic with the pages of the deposition that "control" that point. Specific language the witness chose at their deposition ("Mr. Felmly, I do not have a clue where my notes might be; I have looked high and low") is noted ("not a clue," "high and low"). Having these references in hand is helpful when the witness pulls out the missing notes while testifying on the stand. "Excuse me, Mr. Jones, didn't you tell me at your deposition that you didn't have a *clue* where your notes were located?" (Paralegal simultaneously displays deposition testimony on the monitor.)

Some points of control require careful use of photographs or specialized display techniques demanding careful advanced preparation for cross-examination.

"Dr. Hawthorne" was an environmental scientist testifying for a defendant insurance carrier in a large insurance coverage dispute relating to millions of dollars of environmental clean-up costs incurred by my utility company client. He purported to also be an expert on interpreting aerial photographs, and had testified at deposition that certain aerial photos from the 1940s or 1950s showed pools of liquid tar dumped on the property. He opined that these were evidence of intentional dumping by the plant operator—my client's predecessor company. He stated his

opinion very strongly in the direct examination, using a projected image of that photo.

During the lunch break before my cross, my paralegal and I remained in the courtroom projecting at various levels of enlargement the "black areas" on the photo that Dr. Hawthorne claimed were pools of tar. These were old aerial photos, but with the trial presentation software, we could generate enormous enlargement. (Think today of using Google Earth to try to read the license plate on your car in your driveway.) The following dialogue is drawn from my memory, not the exact transcript, but it went essentially like this:

Mr. Felmly: Dr. Hawthorne, as I understand it, you have, prior to trial, worked with these photos and claimed to have some skill from your military experience many years ago, in the interpretation of aerial photos?

Dr. Hawthorne: Yes, we discussed that at my deposition, and it is an area of expertise that I have. And I did carefully examine these photos, using those skills.

Mr. Felmly: So as we look at the screen and at this photo of the plant during its period of operation, do I understand you to say that these several dark areas that I am noting here with the laser pointer are interpreted by you to be pools of tar? These right here? (Pointing with the laser pointer).

Dr. Hawthorne: Yes. I don't know what else they could be. The plant produced tar, as a by-product, and it seems clear to me that the tar was simply dumped by the operator in this area.

Mr. Felmly: Does this enlargement that my assistant is now making of the photo help us see this a little bit better? (Image enlarged moderately).

Dr. Hawthorne: Yes, I think so; it looks like a pool of tar that you are focusing on.

Mr. Felmly: How about now—now this is quite a bit larger? Does it still seem to you to be a pool of tar?

Dr. Hawthorne: Well, as you enlarge these things, as you know, you do get some further definition of the image of course.

Mr. Felmly: Jane, would you please continue to enlarge that dark area that Dr. Hawthorne and are discussing, and please enlarge it right up to the maximum enlargement capacity of the laptop and the projector? Thank you. (Image is enlarged so that the "black area" largely fills the screen).

Mr. Felmly: (Pausing for 5–10 seconds). Dr. Hawthorne, now looking at this dark area that we've enlarged, and focusing your attention on it and trying to bring to bear your interpretation of this photo, tell me . . . . is that a Studebaker? (Laughter in the courtroom).

Dr. Hawthorne: (Chuckling) I do not know that, Mr. Felmly, but I would agree with you that it appears to be a vehicle. You understand that I did not have available to me equipment that could subject this image to such high magnification and resolution.

Mr. Felmly: And these other dots that we see next to the car, aren't there people standing there apparently about to get into the car?

Opportunities for such theatrics in a courtroom are rare and must be cautiously employed lest the judge or the jury react badly. This jury did not react badly and thought it was wonderful. Dr. Hawthorne had worn out his welcome with the jury before we even began this exercise and he never could recover as a witness.

Cross-examination demands limiting the areas that you will cover, providing airtight control points lest the witness attempt to turn around the examination on you, or to claim a lack of knowledge that will frustrate the exam. Adverse witnesses thrive on (1) changing their story from what they've said before, (2) not remembering, and (3) surprising you with some bombshell not covered in their earlier discovery. Your control must cover all these areas with reference to their deposition or prior statements. Even then, limit the examination to critical points and plan it well in this period prior to trial.

Management of witness outlines and their use at trial are, of course, a matter of personal style and practice. I use three-ring binders containing my witness outlines. I write big on each page of filler paper so that I can read the outline from 3 to 4 feet away, liberating me from the podium, if the judge permits me to move in the courtroom. The cross-examination outline will be prepared a week or more before trial and placed in the binder, but the actual exam at trial will almost always require significant adjustment in the nature or order of presentation of key points on cross. Even the most critical of cross-examinations should rarely have more than ten topical points. Some of them may take an hour to develop, but most will be far shorter. They will be a blend of (1) points of helpful agreement; (2) collateral attack on credentials, ability to recall or observe; (3) inconsistent statements; (4) attack on assumptions underlying opinions; (5) targeted challenge to key case issues; (6) evidence of being over-lawyered or over-prepared as a witness; (7) implications of collateral gain (money, friendship, ideology); and, with luck, a big finish. It is not a time to chat about the case with an adverse witness. It is a time to make key points and get the witness off the stand.

Trial lawyers who seem to conduct their cross-examination from the yellow legal pad on which they wrote their notes during the witness's direct examination constantly amaze me. They must have really liked my direct outline for the witness. Some use a ruler to create a 2.5" column on each page setting out the space for their cross-examination points. It is, of course, essential to listen intensely to the direct, noting either new points to add to the outline, or to supplement or revise existing points. However, the placement, order of presentation, and even the content should not be driven by the order of direct topics on direct. Legal pads with their notes of the direct examination are helpful, but only as they are used to capture comments to refine, or adjust the sequence of presentation of points that are already in your outline for cross-examination and set in the three-ring binder.

When I am conducting a direct exam and I hear behind me at counsel table, the opening of binder rings, I know my opponent (1) has a prepared cross-examination outline, and (2) is in the process of revisiting the order of presentation. Both of these thoughts impress upon me that the cross-examination is likely to be thorough. It is also possible, since my views on this are so well known in the circles in which I travel, that they are simply popping the rings open just to drive me crazy. . .

Witness School

Armed with a solid, but flexible, direct examination outline, you must meet with your client/witness and prepare them to give their evidence, tell their story, and do so accurately, credibly, and, hopefully, with a pleasant demeanor. Preparation for their courtroom testimony involves reviewing the factual story or basis for their opinions, and matching it with the integration of that testimony or story as the foundation for offering the exhibits that will be presented at trial through their testimony. Avoid the temptation to rehearse the exact manner of description or exact script they will provide in telling their story. If you err here they will, in fact, sound scripted and be unpersuasive. In general, you want the witness to put the testimony in their own words, and generally the precise words chosen need not be memorized by the witness. I often explain to witnesses that during their direct examination, it is almost impossible for them to screw up. It is like going to the batting cage and hitting pitches—if I throw a pitch, and they miss, I will re-throw the pitch. And I will handle it so that it appears natural that they missed it. If necessary, I will adjust the pitching machine to throw slower, higher, lower—nothing can go wrong. It is, of course, more complicated than that, but they love hearing that.

The real meat of witness preparation is not rehearsing the factual story on direct examination; it is teaching and empowering the witness to deal with cross-examination. This requires careful discussion and planning for the areas of weakness, or likely impeachment. It is critical to evaluate and address how the witness appears, or presents—are they responsive and credible, or defensive and unbelievable? It is beyond the scope of this handbook to detail all the techniques, tips, and dilemmas that make up preparing a witness for cross-examination, and you must fashion your guidance and style in training so that it is uniquely applicable to each witness's level of confidence, emotions, and ability to operate under stress. Some of these efforts with particular witnesses will present remarkable challenges.

I was defending a young emergency room physician who had been dragged into an ongoing medical negligence case arising out of a medication overdose death of a teenager. There were strong allegations of negligence involving the primary care doctor and others, but by the time this tragedy reached the emergency room, the situation was hopeless. My client's care was actually flawless, and he could not save the boy. The negligence claim against him was plainly the worst thing to ever happen to him in his life and he was completely devastated. He was simply terrified of the entire legal process.

The first witness preparation session for his deposition was truly unprecedented. He called me from the highway a half hour or so before our appointment, explaining that he was in a panic attack, and at an interstate rest stop and he could not drive to his appointment with me. We made arrangements to have someone get him home. He was unable to function with the idea of being subjected to cross-examination on this tragedy, or to even prepare for it.

Multiple sessions over the next week occurred and slowly began to build his confidence. I increasingly role-played the cross-examination he would face. Ultimately, by the third session or so, I assured him that no lawyer would ever be more difficult than I had been in his practice examination.

His deposition in a week or so went well. His skill and his caring for this child came across strongly. He was a very decent man and an excellent doctor. He was very responsive to questioning, respectful, and consistently made reference to the detailed elements of his care, which he had explained in detail in early portions of the deposition. He had a very short story to tell and it was very tragic, but he had done his work well.

He was dropped from the lawsuit shortly after the deposition. He also never forgot that experience and for many years he has stayed in touch, usually at holidays or upon some professional accomplishment, writing a note to reference our experience together. Witness preparation sometimes makes all the difference.

Witness preparation for courtroom testimony should stress at least four critical skills or techniques:

1. **Responsiveness.** Answer the question, then explain. Answer the question, then explain. At least half of all people respond to questions by trying to put the issue or topic in context, or lay some foundation, before they directly answer your question. ("Counsel, in order to explain whether that actually happened to Mary Smith, I must first explain how the valves in the human heart work . . ."). Teach your witness not to do that—answer first, then explain. Setting a context, laying parameters, or giving a mini-lecture on neurosurgery may work for Nobel laureates, but it drives trial lawyers, judges, and, I think, jurors, nuts. Most lawyers do not stress it, and do

not cover it as a teaching point with their witnesses, but you should not ignore it. Answer, then explain.

2. **Dealing with leading questions.** Leading questions terrify your witnesses. They fear them from seeing them on television and they do not know whether they can qualify their responses ("What if she makes me say "yes" or "no?"). Spend a lot of time on this. Empower your witness to provide a credible, fair, and common sense qualification to an overstated or argumentative leading question. Do not encourage quibbling or strident staying on message. Teach them how to spot and neutralize the hyperbole, argument, or even mean-spiritedness of a tough leading question. They should answer and then explain the manner in which it is overstated or inappropriate. ("Yes, part of what you say is true, sir, I *was* at home that day, but it is not true that I should have heard any unusual noises. I was in the basement building a cabinet and cutting wood with a circular saw all morning . . . ").

3. **Dealing with surprise.** Unless your witness is living some remarkable web of lies, there should be nothing in the cross that will dismantle the witness. Be sure you ask, however, "Is there anything in your [background, credentials, professional standing, family relationships . . .] that I need to worry about, that may go bump in the night?" If the answer is "Yes, as a matter of fact there is," then you need to discuss it, but it will not be a surprise. If no, teach the witness calmness, reflection, and a thoughtful, careful response to an unexpected line of questioning. The witness calmly putting the issue raised in context settles almost all surprise lines of cross-examination.

4. **Impeachment from a prior statement or deposition.** You should be alert and work with the witness on any troublesome prior statements or unhelpful references they made

in their deposition. If they are truly bad, most often you should bring them out on direct. As noted above, educate the witness about impeaching statements pulled out of context. If they are able to set or correct the context, that is fine, but also explain that you will deal with the harmful impacts of out-of-context statements when you do your re-direct examination.

Make sure the witness knows the critical themes of the case and can articulate them. If difficult questions are being experienced, these themes will operate as "safe harbors," refuges where the witness can go and put the question in context and survive the ordeal—at least until you can clean things up on re-direct.

Logistics

As you prepare for the final push to trial, you and your team need to assemble the physical components of the case, handle all the housekeeping for a one- to two-week event, and perform all of these functions in good humor, reserving your strength and emotions for the struggle ahead. A system, a plan, and experience play a role in preserving your enthusiasm, vigor, and focus during this final phase of preparation. The following areas or issues should be considered as part of this preparation.

- **Locate the file in a specific place or room for coordinated team preparation.** If you have the luxury of space, develop a case preparation room of dedicated space for exhibit assembly, preparing last minute pleadings, and organizing trial equipment and materials. Reserve the space and keep others out of it.
- **Reserve accommodations for your witnesses, experts, and your trial team, for those trials that demand overnight stays.**

Some venues require this be done quite far in advance of trial. Work out the hotel arrangements, airfare, and ground transport for experts and others so that they can get to court. Avoid hiring limousines to deliver experts and witnesses to the courthouse. Use cabs and simple car services. If your team is staying out of town, consider or investigate whether your opponents are staying in the same hotel. That never works out very well, but is sometimes inevitable. Try to arrange for business service facilities to prepare memoranda, pleadings, and related work necessary during trial. If you have local counsel, try to get a key to their offices for evening preparation. If possible, bring your own printer and do it at the hotel.

- **Organize all equipment and practice with it.** Make sure you can zoom on your document camera, and coordinate display instructions with your team member operating the trial presentation software. If you are dependent on court-supplied equipment, practice with it and understand who to call when it shuts down or breaks. It will.

- **Organize all depositions and deposition abstracts.** Put all deposition abstracts into a "Deposition Abstract Notebook" so they are currently available, either in hard copy or electronic format. They are a great resource for factual information.

- **Prepare a Trial Notes Notebook in a three-ring binder, pages consecutively Bates-stamped.** There is, of course, going to be a transcribed record of your trial, but it will not catch every chambers conference, nor is it available to you in trial unless you are getting daily copy. If you have daily copy available, there is often a day or two delay before you get it. You need an accurate set of trial notes maintained in one place. When several lawyers are examining, handling different witnesses, the Trial Notes Notebook should be passed between the note takers. It will be invaluable as you prepare for Final Argument.

Take Care of Yourself

The last ten days before the trial are commonly characterized by intense activity, long days and nights of work, and considerable apprehension and worry. As you enter this period, try to integrate and schedule family or personal time to moderate this pressure. The means, timing, and activities chosen by you to accomplish this, will depend on your personal circumstances, but avoid the temptation to handle the run-up to trial by putting in two weeks of unrelenting 15-hour days. You will end up exhausted and burned out before the trial even begins and, if replicated case after case over an entire career, you and your family will pay an unacceptable cost. Break up the work day, including weekend days, into segments. Include family and activity time. Start early each day, schedule a 12-hour work period for the case in several blocks of time, and try to preserve meal times with the family, go to children's ball games or recitals, and work off a plan and schedule. Encourage your team members to follow the same course.

Chapter 6

Day 3 to Day 0

The Final Weekend

Assuming your case commences on a Monday, your Final Weekend should be devoted to assembly of your trial exhibits, organizing the file, testing equipment, and polishing your Opening Statement, voir dire, and initial witness outlines.

Assembly of the File

Your trial file will consist of a number of "banker" boxes organized for rapid access to materials in the stress of the trial setting, together with various notebooks discussed above which will contain your outlines and presentations. The assembly of the boxes and the contents should anticipate what materials you will need to take from the courtroom at the end of each trial day. Basic administrative materials, correspondence, notes, drafts, and legal research will likely be left overnight in the courtroom. Most often you can make arrangements to stack your boxes against the courtroom rail, out of the way of early morning motion litigants. The bailiffs will want to lock up the courthouse at 4:30 p.m. sharp, so you need to grab the materials needed for the evening preparation and exit quickly after the trial day ends.

For most cases I suggest the following organization of the boxes:

(a) Pleadings and administrative materials (leave unnecessary administrative materials at the office).

(b) Discovery materials, interrogatories, and responses to document requests. Hopefully, much of this material is available on a laptop in word-searchable format during trial.

(c) Witnesses and depositions. Set this box up sequentially by the order of appearance of witnesses to eliminate lugging multiple witness boxes home each day.

(d) Exhibits.

(e) Research materials, medical treatises, and periodicals.

(f) Your Trial Notebook, with all witness outlines, is in your briefcase. It goes with you each night. It should also contain strategic notes, such as thoughts for the final argument.

You should also consider how you and your team are going to transport the boxes. On the first day of trial, as you bring everything in, you will likely require a "dolly," cart, or luggage totes. Hopefully there will be a courthouse elevator.

Provisioning

You should bring to trial office supplies and equipment aids essential to a week-long trial. Put them in a provisioning and supplies box. Office supplies include pens, pads, Post-It notes, poster board pads, easels, extension cords, and adapter plugs for your trial presentation materials. You should determine how switching the electronic presentation appliances from document camera to the laptop projector will be handled and have the necessary appliance adapter switches for that purpose. Bring masking tape for securing wiring on the floor and any necessary projection lamps, if one burns out. Your provisioning box should include water in plastic bottles, and in my trials, a block of peanut butter crackers, for that period of the day other people describe as "lunch." You should bring the Rules of Evidence and the Rules of Court.

Polishing the Opening

In major cases, it is likely that you will have already presented your opening to your co-counsel and to your client team, especially if you are working with corporate in-house counsel. Even in smaller cases, you will likely have provided it in a moot court setting to your team, encouraging their input and critique. It is important you know how long it will take, measured against the court rule on time. If you are using PowerPoint or projected visuals, be sure you practice the presentation with the visuals. The use of visuals tends to lengthen a presentation. Of course, the goal is to use your notes or outline as a guide, and practice until you are comfortable presenting your opening without reading it. If you are using PowerPoint slides with outlined arguments, they should be simple, uncluttered, and limited in number. The use of the PowerPoint slides, especially if you can see the monitor from your location, will also free you from your notes on the podium. It is not effective to be constantly looking over your shoulder at PowerPoint slides being displayed behind you. Consider the possibility of objections by opposing counsel during your opening. They are far more common now than years ago. Nothing terrible happens when people object, but you should be prepared to handle them in stride.

The Morning of the Trial

Start early. Set two alarms. You will sleep better knowing that you cannot oversleep. Arrange your schedule to arrive at the courthouse an hour or so before the stated time. It takes time to get your boxes into the courtroom and get set up. Introduce yourself and your team to the court reporter, bailiffs, and other staff. Learn their names. Greet opposing counsel warmly, if relations in the case permit that. Welcome your clients as they arrive and then orient them to the courtroom and the courthouse facilities.

Organize your blowups, technology, and other equipment if it can be done prior to drawing the jury. Get your voir dire notes and charts organized, and have all materials necessary for jury selection handy.

It is likely the court will commence the trial by asking you to introduce yourself and your clients to the jury. Introduce all members of your team. Scratch a note with correct pronunciation of clients and co-counsel if those names are challenging to pronounce. Turn and face the jury panel as you make your introduction and look happy to be there.

Just before the proceeding starts, as you are awaiting the entrance of the judge and the words "All Rise" to be announced, take the deepest breath you can draw into your lungs and hold it for 20 to 30 seconds. Then exhale quietly and slowly. An actor friend once told me to do that—it seems to work. You are ready to go.

Several months ago we were driving to a motion hearing in a northern county, pacing ourselves behind school buses bringing the kids from these foothill towns to school, adding to the 2 hours of the trip. It was "mud season" in New Hampshire, with remnant snow piles under the deep firs, people starting to rake out their gardens, the occasional maple syrup bucket hanging on trees, and, of course, mud. My colleague was driving; I was reviewing my notes for the motion argument, until we came to that stretch of road, and a long, sweeping turn through the pasture, now gray, drab, and even cold—far from the way it was bursting with green in mid-August, 1993—on the last day of the most difficult trial of my life. I have taken this road to court many times since that day in 1993, always recalling that day as I pass this spot. I feel the catch in my throat, the emotions of that day flooding in, as it profiled so much about the costs and joys of trial work. . .

The trial had taken five weeks, long over the estimate—enough to dismantle a planned family vacation. It was hard fought. Everything about it was hard. Rulings on evidence had changed repeatedly. The client presented with emotional and medical impairments. The facts, legal issues, witnesses. . . everything about it took all we had to present it well. Two ambulances came to the courthouse during a low point to assist my client.

The fourth day of jury deliberations began with tension and expectation of a verdict. The bailiffs were anxious—everyone just knew. Right after the noon break, opposing counsel took me for a walk and made a seven-figure offer of settlement, requiring an immediate response. Within an hour of my rejection of the offer, we were called into court and the judge opened the verdict. The jury awarded my client a multiple of the recently rejected offer, indeed the exact amount that I requested as a fair verdict in my closing argument to the jury.

After the handshakes, hugs, tears, and goodbyes, I traveled alone down that road, the weight of a thousand worlds lifted from my shoulders—sun roof open, literally flying through the countryside in the full blossom of summer, working the gears of the car through each curve, just relishing the moment. In the stretch of highway approaching the long pasture and curve, a minivan was ahead of me on the road, traveling about half of my speed, clearly occupied by several men. After the curve, I came up close behind to pass, realizing at that moment that at least one of the occupants was a juror from my trial. Weighing the level of appropriate celebration for the moment, I accelerated up beside them, pleased to see three smiling jurors, one of which raised a fist of solidarity and celebration to me, which I returned up through the open sunroof as I passed—not missing a beat on the three-part harmonies I was providing the Indigo Girls as they sang, "Galileo."

We had spent a unique time together, they knew exactly what we went through, and they too celebrated the verdict.

I am sure my colleague wondered at my odd smile and distraction as we passed that spot several months ago, taking in the memories of that day, and so much more.

About the Author

Bruce W. Felmly is a trial lawyer with over forty years' experience who chairs the Litigation Department at New Hampshire's largest law firm—McLane, Graf, Raulerson & Middleton, P.A. He joined that firm as an associate in 1972, after graduation from Cornell Law School. Bruce and his wife, Susan, live in Manchester, New Hampshire, as well as in a lakeside cabin in the Western Mountains of Maine on Rangeley Lake. They have three children and six grandchildren.

Bruce has spent his entire career in trial practice, in the early years trying a large number of plaintiff's personal injury cases and developing a specialty in medical malpractice claims. Over the years his practice expanded, focusing more on environmental claims, products liability cases, and a wide array of land use claims, employment disputes, and energy-related litigation. He has extensive experience in the courtroom, having tried scores of cases, most of them to juries.

Bruce was honored to serve as the President of the New Hampshire Bar Association in 1995 to 1996, and was elected a Fellow to the American College of Trial Lawyers in 1990. From 2006 to 2010, he served on the Board of Regents of the American College of Trial Lawyers. He is an elected member of the American Law Institute, has served multiple terms on the New Hampshire Board of Bar Examiners, and chaired the New Hampshire Supreme Court Long-Range Strategic Planning Effort for the Court System in 2003.

He is an active participant in the Inns of Court, New Hampshire Pro Bono Program, and numerous community and professional organizations. He is frequently called upon to teach attorneys in the area of trial practice and has written a number of articles and publications on that topic.

Bruce is an avid fly fisherman, bird hunter, and guitar player.

Index

A

Abstracts of depositions, 88

Accepted standards of care, 76

Accommodations, reserving, 87

Adapters, for different devices, 20, 92

Administrative materials, 92

Adverse witness, 78, 81

Alarms, 93

Animations, 14

B

Backup laptops, 19

Backups, 19

Bar codes, 22

Bench book, 15, 43

Binders, using, 82, 88

Blowups, 16, 93

Boxes, organizing files in, 91–92

Broad introductory witnesses, 75

Burnout, avoiding, 89

C

Cabs, hiring, 87

Car services, 87

Cases

difficult or damaging aspects of, 76

model for discussion, 5–6

problems, 69

putting into shape (day 60 to day 30), 79–80

status, settlement, and problems, 69

Cell phones, 59, 69

Challenges for causes, 61

Checklist, 3, 4

Circumstances, vs. primacy, 75

Claims, waiver of, 42–43

Clients. *See also* witnesses

demeanor in courthouse, 69

interactions with witnesses, 68–69

personal meetings with, 65–67

preparing for trial, 65–67

respect of the role and service of jury, 68

role at trial, 67

scheduling, 8–9, 51

Clients (*continued*)
  timeliness and attendance
    throughout trial, 67
  visibility in courtroom and
    to jury, 67
Closing arguments. *See
  also* opening
  statements
  timing of, 40–41
Cloud storage, 19
Confidential information,
  handling, 64
Connecticut, xii
Counterclaims, 10
Courthouses
  arrival in (morning of
    trial), 93
  client visibility in, 67
  demeanor of clients in, 69
  demonstrative re-creation
    in, 13
  explaining facilities to
    clients, 66
  permission to access in
    advance, 20
Courtroom technology,
  evaluating, 20
Cross-examination.
    See also direct
    examination
  binders in, using, 82
  dealing with surprise in,
    86
  documents for, 64
  exhibits, 20, 64

motions in limine and, 47
of expert witnesses, 12
outlines, 74–76
photographs in, 79–80
preparing client/witness
  for, 84
preparing witnesses for,
  83–85
technology and, xi
vignette, 84–85

D
Damages, itemization in
    pretrial statements, 33
Day 3 to day 0 (trial
    preparation), 91
Day 3 to day 0 (trial
    preparation)day 03
  assembly of trial file,
    91–92
  morning of trial, 93–94
  polishing the opening,
    93–94
  provisioning, 92–94
  vignette, 94–96
Day 10 to day 3 (trial
    preparation), 71
  logistics, 87–88
  preparing for jury
    selection, 71–74
  preparing your witness,
    74–76
  taking care of yourself, 89
Day 20 to day 10 (trial
    preparation), 57

marking exhibits in, 63–64
preparing clients for trial, 65–67
pretrial conference, 57–58
resolving objections in, 63–64
Day 30 to day 20 (trial preparation), 29
depositions to be presented to jury, 38–40
exhibit lists, 37–38
motions in limine, 45–47
preparing draft of opening statement, 53–54
pretrial filings, 31–33
pretrial statements, 32–34
proposed jury instructions, 43–44
prospects for settlement, 41–42
requests for findings of fact and rulings of law, 44–45
requests related to voir dire, 48–50
special verdict form, 43–45
timing of opening statements and closing arguments, 40–41
trial counsel, 42–43
views, 34–35
vignette, 29

waiver of claims or defenses, 42–43
witness lists, 40–42
Day 60 to day 30 (trial preparation), 7
demonstrative evidence, 13–14
focus groups, 26–27
insurance, 26–27
mediation, 24–25
mock trials, 26–27
presentation techniques, 15–17
putting the case into shape, 10–12
scheduling, 8–9
settlement, 24–25
vignette, 7–8
"Day in the life" films, 14
Defenses, waiver of, 42–43
Demonstrative evidence, xii, 13–14
Depositions. *See also* evidence; witnesses
abstracts, 88
editing, 21
formatting, 21
impeachment from, 86
in impeachment process, 79
organizing, 88, 92
scheduling, 53
to be presented to jury, 38–40

Depositions (*continued*)
use of, 60
Direct examination. *See
also* cross-examination
exhibits, 20
notes, 82
outlines, 74–76
photographs in, 79
preparing client/witness
for, 83–85, 86
Discovery
accessibility through
laptop, 21
organizing, 92
Document camera, 17–18,
18, 88, 92

E
Electronic presentation aids,
59, 92
Elmo projection, 17–18, 22,
77
E-mail, 59
Equipment
Elmo projection, 17–18,
22, 77
organizing and practicing
with, 88
organizing prior to jury
drawing, 94
Errors of judgment, 43
Evidence
blowups, 16
demonstrative, xii, 13–14
electronically stored, 3

Federal Rule of Evidence,
64
final pretrial conference
and, 60
in direct and cross-
examination
outlines, 74–76, 75,
76, 77, 78, 82
in exhibit lists, 37, 38
in proposed jury
instructions, 43
mixed media, 19
motions in limine and, 32,
45–47, 48
opening statement and,
53–54
pre-marked exhibits, 16
presenting, 15–17
pretrial statement and,
32–35
requests for findings of
fact and rulings of
law, 44
testing in mock trials/focus
groups, 26–27
use of technology in,
17–18
views and, 34, 35, 36–38
Exhaustion, avoiding, 89
Exhibits
creating instantly available
displays of, 20
lists, 37–38, 77
marking, 63–64
organizing, 92

pre-marked, 16
workbook of, 15
Experts. *See also* witnesses
cross-examination of, 12
opinions, solidifying and
refining, 11
reserving accommodations
for, 87
scheduling, 50
transportation of, 87
vignette, 79–80
Extension cords, 20

F
Facebook, 73
Federal Rule of Evidence, 64
Federal Rules of Civil
Procedure F.R.C.P.
26(e)(2), 11
Files
assembly of, 91–92
confidential, 64
locating, in specific place
or room, 87
organizing in boxes, 91–92
Final pretrial conference,
57–58
Final weekend. *See* day
3 to day 0 (trial
preparation)
Findings of fact, requests for,
44–45
Focus groups, 26–27

G
Government investigators,
74

H
Hearsay, 37
Hotels, 87

I
Impeachment, 79
documents for, 64
of witnesses, 86
Instinctive action doctrine,
34
Insurance, 26–27
Internet, 72–74
iPads, 19

J
Jury
asking questions during
views, 36
client's respect of role and
service of, 68
depositions to, 37
instructions, 60
introducing client and trial
team to, 94
note-taking by, 59
proposed instructions for,
43–44
questions by, 59
Jury selection, 62
consultants, 73
mechanics of, 61

Jury selection (*continued*)
  preparing for, 71–74
  questionnaires, 71
  scheduling, 52
  social media tools and, 73
  voir dire, 48–50

K
Key witnesses
  preparing, 74
  scheduling, 52

L
Lash drives, 19
Leading questions, dealing
  with, 86
Lead-off witness, 75
Legal claims, assessing for
  viability, 8
LinkedIn, 73
Lip charts, 23
Litigation technology, 3
"Little people", xi
Local counsel, role of, 60
Logistics, 87–88

M
Manchester, New
  Hampshire, 1
Massachusetts, xii
Media operators, 22
Mediation, 24–25
Medical bills, 38

Medical damages,
  itemization in pretrial
  statements, 33
Medical negligence, xi,
  84–85
Medical probability, 76
Medical records, 12, 16,
  37–38, 45, 76, 78
Medical treatises, 92
Meetings
  calendaring, 3
  team, 3
  with client representatives,
    65
  with clients, 66
  with insurance carriers, 26
  with witnesses, 74
Missouri, xii
Mixed media, 19, 23
Motions in limine, 32, 45–47
Movie clips, 3–4

N
Negligence
  instructions on, 43
  medical, 84–85
  professional, 76–78
New Hampshire, xi, 1, 8
New Hampshire Trial Bar
  News, 2
New York, xii
Nurses, xi

O
Objections, resolving, 63–64

Office supplies, 92
Opening statements.
    See also closing
    arguments; pretrial
    statements
    outlining, 55
    polishing, 93–94
    preparing draft of, 53–54
    timing of, 40–41
Overnight stays, 87

P
Paralegals, 3
Periodicals, 92
Phones, 59, 69
Photographs, 36, 79–80
Pleadings, 92
Police officers
    as witnesses, xi, 32, 51
    preparing as witness, 74
    reports, 37
Police report, 37, 78
PowerPoint, 18–20, 67, 93
Presentation techniques,
    15–17
    blowups, 16
    kits, 20
    mixed media, 19
    pre-marked exhibits, 16
    vendors or consultants, 19
    video projector, 17–18
Pretrial conference, final,
    57–58
Pretrial filings, preparing,
    31–33

Pretrial management
    conference, 31
Pretrial package, 32
    pretrial statement, 32–34
    proposed jury instructions,
        43–44
    requests for findings of
        fact and rulings of
        law, 44–45
    special verdict form,
        43–45
Pretrial statements, 32–34
    exhibit lists, 37–38
    opening statements,
        40–41, 53–54,
        93–94
    waiver of claims or
        defenses in, 42–43
    witness lists, 40–42
Pre-view statement, 34
Primacy, vs. circumstances,
    75
Product liability, xi, 45
Professional negligence,
    76–78
Projection bulbs, 20
Properties, viewing, 36
Provisioning, 92–94

Q
QR codes, 22

R
Reasonable medical
    certainty, 76

Requests for findings of fact
and rulings of law,
44–45
Research materials, 92
Reservations, 87
Responders, 74
Responsiveness of witnesses,
85
Rules of Court, 92
Rules of Evidence, 92
Rulings of law, requests for,
44–45

S
Scheduling, 8–9
  charts, 51
  clients, 51
  experts, 50
  trial, 50–52
  witnesses, 50–52
Sequestration of witnesses,
61
Settlement
  informing clients about, 69
  negotiations for, 24–25
  prospects for, 41–42
Smart phones, 59, 69
Snacks, 92
Social media, 73
Software for trial
  preparation, 18
South Carolina, xii
Special damages, itemization
  in pretrial statements,
33

Special verdict forms, 43–45,
60
Struck jurors, 61
Surprises, dealing with, 86

T
Tablets (electronic device),
19
Teamwork, 3–4
Transportation, 87
Trial
  mock, 26–27
  morning of, 93–94
  preparing clients for,
    65–67
  scheduling, 8–9, 50–52
  vignette, 94–96
Trial counsel, 42–43
Trial management
  conference, 31
Trial notes notebook, 88, 92
Trial preparation
  balance and, 4–5
  day 3 to day 0, 91
  day 10 to day 3, 71
  day 20 to day 10, 57
  day 30 to day 20, 29
  day 60 to day 30, 7
  setting stage for, 1
  vignette, 1–3
Trial presentation software,
18
Trial team
  introducing members of,
    94

reserving accommodations
for, 87

V
Vanishing trial, ix
Verdict forms, 43–45, 60
Viability, claims for, 10
Video depositions
editing, 21
formatting, 21
scheduling, 53
to be presented to jury,
38–40
use of, 60
Videographers
editing of video
depositions, 21
working with, 14
Video projector, 17–18
Views, 34–35
Voir dire, 48–50, 59, 94

W
Water bottles, 92
Watergate, 48–50
Winslow, Arizona, 1
Witnesses. *See also* clients;
experts
adverse, 78, 81

broad introductory, 75
case vignette, 79–80
cross-examination
outlines, 74–76
direct examination
outlines, 74–76
impeachment from prior
statement or
deposition, 86
interactions with clients,
68–69
key, 74
leading questions, dealing
with, 86
lead-off, 75
lists of, 40–42
personal meetings with,
65–67
preparing, 74–76
reserving accommodations
for, 87
responsiveness of, 85
running out of, 53
scheduling, 8–9, 50–52
sequestration of, 61
surprises, dealing with, 86
transportation of, 87
vignette, 67